THINK LIKE AN ODD FELLOW!

Wisdom and self-improvement in 21st Century Odd Fellowship

Think Like An Odd Fellow!

By R. Scott Moye

ISBN:
978-0-578-93059-6

CONTENTS

INTRODUCTION

This book is based on many of the earlier works on Odd Fellowship.

The older works of Odd Fellowship are written in a difficult to read style. I decided to take parts of the old Odd Fellows works along with similar works of the late 19th century, update the language, include 21st-century concepts, mix them with the 19th-century ones, and put them in book form. The writing style still has elements of the 19th century, to keep a more "ancient" feel to the book.

The older works all contained elements of what today we would call self-improvement and community action. This book is a blending of the old and new. It is written in a short and concise style to make it a quicker read.

If you've read the older works on Odd Fellowship, you'll find many parts of them here. Some sections in this work contain paragraphs from several different Odd Fellows books blended to create a more cohesive understanding of the older principles. In some cases, a paragraph is made from sentences taken from several separate sections in several different 19th-century Odd Fellows writings. I felt it was essential to use information from older works to adhere to the Order's principles. The main book used as the basis for this work is *Odd Fellows Pocket Companion* of 1867 by Ridgely and Donaldson.

HOW TO USE THIS BOOK
The book has 42 entries or essays. I recommend reading the book from beginning to end. Once that is done, you may wish to start at the beginning and read one entry per day as a daily reading.

Edited by Margo Gifford, 2021

Written during the world-wide pandemic, 2020-2021

1. OUR DEGREES

I am grateful for my existence. I rejoice that I have a place amid the bright-robed mysteries which surround me. I glory in the shifting scenery of the seasons. No flaw do I find in the sun, the moon, or the stars. No prayer have I to make that the grass which grows at my feet may be fairer than it is, or that the mornings and evenings may be more attractive. Let me know as I may, and feel as I should, the truth that I am endlessly improvable, and I am assured that the universe will somehow sweeten every bitter allotment that falls to me. That it will "charm my pained steps over the burning marl," which belongs to the course of temporary experience, and it will assist me joyfully to approach the greatness of nature's own infinite and tranquil character.

It is bliss to feel that the universal love sought by humans is an ever-enduring entity. Unlike the clouds and the snow-heaps, the fluids and the liquids, the rocks, and the metals—unlike all the generations of living organisms—universal love neither wastes away nor loses

1

its distinctiveness. Nay, it outlasts every transmuting process and is endlessly living.

--Excerpt edited from The Jericho Road by W. Bion Adkins, 1899

A critical time in an Odd Fellow's life is passing through the outer door to Odd Fellowship. The obligations and lessons instilled in you as you progress in the Order help develop your intellectual and moral growth. You will learn about the brutality of poverty, the burdens of humanity, and lessons about society. You will be instructed on the instability of wealth and power.

The Independent Order of Odd Fellows is an organization that instructs you on how to help your community and make your life more advantageous and pleasant. It aims to increase the mental and moral strength and improve the compassion of your heart. You must prepare your mind and body for the tasks which you will undertake.

You'll find in these pages the voice of wisdom and truth. You'll learn how to do your duty regarding the universe, the country in which you live, your neighbors, community, your family, and yourself. You'll come to understand it's possible to live with a peaceful and contented mind, which is something people the world over seek. You'll discover that corruption, degeneracy, and evildoing are horrors that should be shunned. You'll learn that when you need fraternal support, unity, and love, it will be there for you. You'll see that people respect those who apply these lessons.

There are two lessons (among others) you learn as an initiate. *First,* there's a contrast of the lodge room with the outside world. In that contrast, it's shown that while conflict and divisions exist in the world, there are none in the lodge because friendship and love mildly assert their dominion. Simultaneously, the ideas of faith and charity blend, blessing the mind with peace and mellowing the heart with sympathy. The entire Order is under the same obligations and practice the same beliefs. *Second*, the Order teaches a lesson on the doctrine of human immorality; humans are captives—chained by our thoughts and emotions, which may throw the learner back to the days of primeval society.

Confession of ignorance is the first step toward discovering truth. As an initiate, you must recognize your ignorance because it makes acquiring knowledge easier. Before you joined the Order, you were unaware of social limitations. You were shackled to sense and emotion. Humans are in moral darkness in their modern natural state, bound with chains of involuntary servitude to greed and selfishness.

You are a captive of a mighty foe, chained, and led at the will of your captors. You're a captive of moral and ethical error—but in ignorance of it. You lack wisdom but don't realize your condition. You're not conscious of your position, your situation, or the danger you are in. You can't see the sword that enforces universal justice is raised above your head. You're like a person in a dark room surrounded by hissing and poisonous insects, who are restlessly crawling about and preparing to empty their poison sack in a fatal sting. But being spiritually deaf and blind you're unaware of the hazard.

Our degrees give striking evidence of humankind's instability, its tendency to death, the grave, and corruption. Death, the mighty conqueror of life, appears in the mind riding through society's ranks, marking its victims for the tomb. Death brings the rich and the poor, the learned and unlearned, the high and low, on to a common level.

Our degrees group before the mind examples from all countries, languages, and peoples, with training in the arts and sciences, who possess different opinions, different faiths and conflicting interests; and it presents the Golden Rule as a base of action for all. Our degrees warn against bigotry and urge sensible toleration. The whole of humanity is one family. Towards one another, they should act on the Golden Rule, "Whatsoever ye would that men should do to you, do ye also even to them." Love and tolerance to all humanity should energize every Odd Fellow.

What if they have different manners, customs, and principles? They're still the creatures of the same universe. All are dependent on the universe, other people, and the principle of general fellowship. True fellowship is the duty and privilege of all humankind.

Faith in others cements society together and forms the endearments of all relationships. Faith is belief based on confidence in another person's integrity, rather than on one's knowledge, reason, or judgment. Faith leads to confidence between people and societies.

No less important is hope, defined to be "expectation of future good." This quality dwells in the heart of every good Odd Fellow. It inspires us with courage for labor and endurance. Throughout the stormy ocean of time, sometimes with the threat of wreck and destruction, hope's anchor, fastened to the cable of faith, holds the vessel secure till the storm is over and gone.

Charity, or love, is another essential pillar. By it we don't mean cold alms-giving. But a pure love that sympathizes with suffering and will bear the severe test of adversity; a love which is an imitation of universal love.

Odd Fellows know that life is a pilgrimage. It begins in infancy and ends, if not before, in old age. The first part of the journey is when childhood gives place to youth's bloom, fire, and energy. The second part is when youth, with all its freshness, beauty, and love, gives place to adulthood and the sterner realities of life. The third is when the apex is reached, and the other side's descent begins. Then "the strong man begins to tremble, the grinders (teeth) cease because they are few, and *those that look out* at the windows (eyes) be darkened." The fourth part is when age and its infirmities have gathered in on the subject until the "grasshopper becomes a burden and desire fails."

2. MORTALITY

You are nothing but a shadow that floats for a moment in time, soon to be consumed by the light of the endless ages. Your ignorance darkens the sight of the universe around you. Your ability to understand the natural world is interfered with by your out of control emotions. The human race assumes we have all the answers, yet, we rarely appreciate the questions.

Until something drastic or horrible affects us, we rarely know just how little wisdom and control we truly have. Your life is brief, and we sometimes perceive ourselves as a guilty survivor after shedding tears over the grave of a loved one. You must realize that death, the worker of tremendous change, will alter your joy into sorrow and sever the most endeared and tender relationships.

Countless mementos of our mortality surround humanity. Today, you may stand at the coffin of an infant. Tomorrow you may see youth in the bloom of life carried to an early grave. Another day you may watch someone else, who, after a long journey through life, sinks at last to rest.

On your brow is stamped the seal of mortality. Decay makes pathways into your own body, and you must be aware that one day the time will come when you will be a tenant of the tomb. "Man comes forth like a flower, and is cut down; he flees as a shadow and continues not."

There will be days you will be saddened when thinking of your past and those who have left your life, and there will be times this will happen amid seasons of hilarity and festivity. Remember that as you sleep the sleep of no earthly waking, you also will be remembered by others who still live.

Odd Fellows understand that death is an instructor. From it, you will learn the lesson of survival, even through hopelessness and despair. Death teaches you to evaluate your strengths. It illustrates that the universe will continue its lessons even though you may wish to quit, and you'll realize all things continue, although change still occurs. That even though you will never forget those you lose, you won't run away from living life. Death shows that there are things you appreciate experiencing in life. These are things you must focus on and emphasize to develop their full potential for a good life. Death underscores not taking people for granted--share your life, be with those you love and who love you back. Death teaches you that change is a universal law. The consuming process of nature can't be subverted, and you can't escape it. All things change.

And know this: when anything begins, the end is always in sight.

Death instructs that it's not always your fault when bad events come to pass. It teaches you to accept the impossible.

Once you accept another's death, you can begin your grieving process. Learning the lesson of acceptance is a central component of contentment. Death can initiate the process of expanding your awareness because it challenges you to question your own life and how you view yourself concerning society, nature, and those you love.

Finally, death prepares us to recognize the most superb phenomena and wonders of life. From connecting to the natural world to connecting with the life force in others, there is beauty, surprise, and hope, every day.

3. SYMMETRY, ASYMMETRY, AND TIME

Odd Fellowship gives you instructions about the natural world. Natural laws and universal Order guide you. You may find that the sense of beauty in the sand and stars isn't only exterior to humans. Natural beauty makes up your mental and physical interior as well. Nature becomes more beautiful when you realize and internalize the knowledge that you're part of the natural world's order and symmetry. You aren't an observer of nature on the outside looking in; you are also inside nature.

In everyday language, symmetry is a sense of harmony and balance. Symmetry may be found in music, architecture, science, nature, and in all of creation. You will find symmetry in the emblems of our Order.

In social interactions involving people and community, which is a focus of Odd Fellowship, you will see that people and societies follow a certain symmetry in their communication and relationships. Cooperation, understanding, apology, conversation, sympathy, respect, and justice are examples of how symmetry and balance work in society and social interactions. The Golden Rule is a prime example of symmetry among people and communities.

The concept of symmetry, or the balanced arrangement of nature, intrigues us because it reflects nature's universal order. Using the idea of symmetry, you will realize that society has progressed from a chaotic to a more ordered environment. Humans recognize patterns and symmetry because that's what we are.

Asymmetry is the opposite of symmetry. At times, it can be base or mean, and asymmetry's allure of a chaotic undercurrent can draw us in. Between people, it sends a message of a terrible power struggle or one person thinking they are more important, unique, or better than another. But asymmetry can also be beautiful.

A knotted and crooked tree, random and oddly formed clouds in the sky, a birthmark, a strand of hair that escapes again and again from behind the ear--these are hauntingly beautiful examples of asymmetry. Asymmetry reminds us of the fragility of life. Like the fruit that becomes sweetest before it spoils, life is all the more precious when we realize how temporary it is.

Symmetrical forms in nature show us the universe persists-- creating new life in its image and striving to assemble an order that will stand up against deterioration. Asymmetry reminds us of these two facts: change and the consuming process of nature. Inevitably all things wear down and fall apart only to be used by the universe again to build new realities.

As composite beings, humans have an animal body, a rational mind, and a life force that animates us. As a result of nature's consuming process, the body will crumble to dust and return to the earth from where it came, either by sudden destruction, infirmities, or old age. Nothing is more uncertain than the life of a human. Our lives are justly compared to grass or dust that wouldn't tip the scale of vanity. For this reason, the character of the Grim Reaper holds a scythe and carries an hourglass to illustrate the mowing down of old and young in the way the grass of the field is cut down.

The crescent moon identifies with the curved shape of the scythe. The waxing crescent moon personifies the planting of crops or the beginning of deeds, events, or circumstances as they increase. The waning crescent moon is the personification of the reaping scythe, or the end of accomplishments, occurrences, or circumstances. Yet again, we see the lesson of change and nature's consuming process.

The story of Jonathan and David, you will note, refers to the waxing crescent moon. In the modern world, the new moon is on "the dark of the moon." However, in ancient times the new moon was the first crescent moon after the dark of the moon.

The hourglass, also carried by the Grim Reaper, is broken into an upper and lower chamber, resembling the figure 8. The figure 8, when tipped on its side, is a symbol of eternity. In Odd Fellowship, the symbol of eternity appears as the hourglass is turned and begins to run. Each grain of sand running through the upper chamber is a moment in time and indicates you can't stay in this earthly realm for long. A tiny portion of time is given to you, and taken away without being noticed. So time is made of smaller moments, and they're continuously running onward. In the time given to you, do all the good in your power, even to your enemies, if possible.

As a child, you spend your time in little pleasures of the type that can't give satisfaction in your riper years. Adolescence is a flower that soon withers, a blossom that soon falls off before we are aware of it. Then, you enter middle age encircled with a thick cloud of cares and find yourself surrounded by pricking thorns of difficulties, after which comes old age along with its train of infirmities. Then we are finally set down at last next door to the grave.

4. CHANGE AND THE SINS OF THE FATHER

Through your years, you will see many solemn changes pass before you. If you're observant, you can profit from the lessons of life. One of the lessons is that the universe won't completely abandon a kind person. If you are good and do all the good you can, even your children and grandchildren will reap the benefits of your conduct.

Remember the "sins of the father" lesson found in many ancient teachings. The lesson is that the wrong committed by a nation, state, society, or family leadership passes down through generations. Poor stewardship of the earth and nature will affect people in the future. War, violence, greed, hatred, forced poverty, lack of education, drug abuse, personal assault, and social dysfunction contribute to creating deplorable conditions for those who come after them. These effects build until the weight becomes too heavy to carry, causing a breakdown in the social or familial contract. Solving these problems only comes with a considerable expense, lots of time, and a community's massive effort.

5. GOODNESS, CORRUPTION, AND HOLDING YOUR PEACE

Conducting yourself as a respectable person will get you the respect of the wise and honest. The example you set will increase the goodness already in your life. If you already have positive things in life, then doubling down on reputable behavior and right thinking will increase them. Also, honorable behavior will increase goodness in unacceptable situations. Good conduct is likely to foster friendliness, generosity, honesty, favoritism, and goodwill in harmful and challenging situations.

Honesty and kindness are admired even by those who are evil. Deception and corruption are despicable even to those who practice them. You can see this when the tables turn, and the evil person complains when someone uses crime against them. In your dealings with humankind, especially with other Odd Fellows, take nothing more than your due and, in all things, avoid any indication of corruption and deception.

You should "be just and fear not." Do not let your fear

of a person induce you to falsehood and corruption. Your conscience should always be permitted to govern you, and as it directs, you should act.

You should be honest with other people by speaking well of them. If you can't speak well of them, then hold your peace. Remaining peaceful will prevent you from becoming known as a backbiter, agitator, or trouble maker. You cannot buy or sell someone's destroyed reputation. The person who steals someone's good reputation receives no profit from it, ultimately.

6. THINGS AND PEOPLE MAY NOT BE WHAT THEY SEEM

Plato, in his book, The Republic, tells us a story about some prisoners chained up in a cave and forced to watch shadows on a stone wall. The prisoners have been living there in chains since they were born. They've never seen the outside world, only shadows of it. The prisoners are chained facing the stone wall and are unable to turn their heads. A fire behind them produces enough light to create shadows on the wall.

Periodically, someone passes between the fire and the prisoners with an animal, furniture, or other object which throws its shadow on the stone wall. The prisoners, because of their chained condition, believe these shadows to be the real thing. They believe the shadow of a horse is really a horse and the shadow of a rabbit is a real rabbit, and that the shadow of a human is really a human. Of course, a shadow of a rabbit, a horse, or a human isn't the thing itself. It's only a shadow.

One day, a prisoner breaks their chains and escapes from the dark cave to the light of the-outside world. What the escapee sees is astonishing. The sun is shining, illuminating everything so the prisoner can now see. In the bright light the world is colorful, full of life, exciting! The escaped prisoner sees what real horses, humans, and rabbits look like and marvels at the reality of their form and color. After thinking about it, the prisoner understands that the shadows in the cave are reflections of reality, not the real thing. Full of truth and love of the real illumined world, the prisoner returns to the cave.

The newly freed prisoner explains life in the real world to the chained prisoners in the cave. The chained prisoners call the escapee mad, insane, delusional. They maintain their shadow reality is the real world. The prisoners become violent when the escapee tries to free them from their chains. They prefer to remain as they are, ignorant of the happiness that awaits them in a better world outside the cave.

Before you became an Odd Fellow you were a prisoner. Once you became an Odd Fellow the path to a better life and a better world for all was revealed to you. Friendship, Love, and Truth illuminate, color, and make for an exciting life. Ponder your initiation well, Odd Fellow...

People are not what they always seem. They may largely deceive you. A poor person with rough hands and humble garb may be generous. In contrast, another person with wealth, manners, and appearance may be base and mean. It would be best if you judge people by their conduct, not by their appearance or profession. A person who has a compassionate and benevolent heart who is willing to do good to others and does not close his hand to society is a true humanitarian.

It can be challenging to see the clues that signal someone is not who they seem. It's best to assume someone has good intentions, but the reality is that this isn't consistently the case. Sometimes people pretend to be benevolent for their own ends. It's essential to spot the telltale signs of this behavior:

False modesty is when someone mentions their accomplishments while bragging too much about themselves at the same time. Speak less of yourself and more about the other person with whom you visit.

People who are overly aggressive but maintain the illusion of a pleasant demeanor may not be who they claim to be. This behavior is the ploy of a corrupt person who has suppressed their anger. They deliver a compliment but are arrogant, biting, and sarcastic as they state it.

Some people show false emotions that don't match an ongoing circumstance. Or, their feelings may be entirely out of context. Sometimes people will alter their emotions quickly from being sad to being hopeful. This is a quick sign they are deceptive.

A reasonable person will listen to what you have to say. A person who isn't concerned about your situation and conditions will have difficulty doing this because they're self-centered. Their thoughts revolve around themselves. They will often try and sway the discussion or discourse back to themselves instead of listening to you.

Someone who may be manipulative will always seem to want something. They slowly steer a conversation to their own needs and desires, all while being cordial and friendly. Then they will ask a favor of you or ask you to lend them something you own.

Beware of those who only act in a positive way toward those who have wealth and power. It is good to judge people by how they treat those less fortunate than themselves. If their friendly behavior is directed solely to those in power or who have wealth, their behavior can be corrupt.

Take care to avoid those who gossip and criticize others for no apparent reason. They gossip about others' misfortune under the disguise of caring about them. If they try and befriend you by attacking others, be vigilant and watchful. Some people attach themselves to those who gossip and criticize. Beware of these people as well.

An honest person will treat those who are often ignored by others and society with respect, appreciation, and decency. The homeless, the poor, the uneducated, the marginalized, those affected by bigotry all receive the best intentions from a tolerant person. You must strive to be honest.

An admirable person will talk about your interests even if it's not a topic that is interesting to them. The key is that they show you they care about who you are and what you think and are interested in building rapport with you. They're generous with sharing their belongings, even if they are very attached to them. You must strive to be admirable.

A dependable person will come to the rescue even if they don't know the whole story. The Good Samaritan did this. A dependable person will step in and try to help people who may not be able to do much for themselves. They are inviting and inclusive and engage quiet people in their conversations. They don't attempt to form a clique to ignore others. They help out even when there's nothing in it for them. You must strive to be dependable.

Most people are, in reality, "on the level." There are fewer deceptive people and many more good ones. Scrutinize and be alert to another's actions and assume they have goodness in their heart until otherwise proven. But here's a real lesson about the list above: how many of these things do you need to change in yourself?

7. CREATING A GOOD SOCIETY IS AN ACT OF LOVE

Loving others is a remedy for social evils. We describe love in different ways. Romantic love is generally a mix of emotional and sexual desire that bonds you to another person. There is friendship love, a shared goodwill with another person who is pleasant and acceptable to you. The type of love between parents, children, and siblings is familial. Universal love is an unselfish concern for the welfare of others and the natural environment. Another type is healthy self-love--not to the point of narcissism, which is a great evil--but of the kind where your self-esteem is steady, and your self-confidence is bold. You should make love your aim and study.

Friendship, Love, and Truth—are golden links that bind Odd Fellows together. They recognize and embrace a kind word and a generous deed committed by any human. Amid the upheavals of communities, the crumbling of nations, systems, and governments, these links don't swerve from their course and aren't corralled by arbitrary boundaries. Whatever the language, nationality, or religion of a person, an Odd Fellow can read on humanity's brow the inscription "a woman and a sister, a man, and a brother."

The principle of Love teaches you the capabilities for goodness, enlightens your mind, enlarges the sphere of your good will, and leads to proper fraternal relations designed by the great author of your existence. Love teaches us to be self-sacrificing. For example, think of the people through history who turned their back on the splendors of fame, wealth, and power and chose to share the wretchedness of an oppressed people rather than serve as a pawn for their oppressors. How bright on the pages of history shine these acts of love and sacrifice.

Love can't belong to one organization, party, or group. Love is mysterious and powerful, and as you have seen, it comes in several forms. It can be made to bud and bloom under the fierce rays of a torrid zone, amid the icebergs of Greenland, or the Caucasus' neverending snows. It carries the same smile, whether in the cabin or the palace. Following in its footsteps is a gentle influence that gathers within its world hostile natures. It controls elements of discord, stills storms, soothes spirits of emotion, and directs human efforts to bring peace to the world.

The making of a society is a work of love and is one of the highest arts. Odd Fellows, because of our community work, must know the importance of healthy societies and how they are composed. Love is the basis of all our community ambitions.

A community, if it works correctly, benefits all who partake in it. What society does and how it treats the less fortunate that belong to it is more important than what it accomplishes for those who already have plenty. What a society becomes is invariably more important than what it achieves. A community should construct parks, houses, hospitals, schools, roads, and new technologies that benefit each member of humanity. These things are essential, so people have places to live, employment, businesses, and have a feeling of security. By doing these things, society teaches individual members the importance of love, mutual support, and caring for its less fortunate members.

Many benefits for humanity come with the idea of social compacts. Social compacts have existed in all nations among all people. We find them in every walk of life, where people bind themselves to each other in various business relations. Governments make treaties or contracts of peace, or people enter into marriage contracts, for instance.

A social compact can also be called a "social contract." In a social contract, a person gives up some of their individuality to the decisions made by a majority. In exchange, the person receives protection and order from society. When you become an Odd Fellow, you're entering a social contract. Still, other than perhaps giving up free time to attend lodge or do charitable work, you're surrendering no individual freedoms. Yet, by joining the Order, you will receive support, life training, and counsel when you need it most.

For social compacts or contracts to exist, there must be a functional social structure. A social structure is a set of agreements that both come from and predetermine an individuals' actions. You affect your community by your actions, and conversely, the activities of the community affect you. A society has sets of rules, social and professional groups, and the roles people fill. Examples of the social structure in a small community are law, economy, class, family, and religion. The overarching structure for a larger society comprises economic systems, legal systems, political systems, and cultural systems. These systems impact the social structure in a smaller society.

As discussed in Plato's Republic, we find the concept of the social contract in antiquity. An ongoing debate about social contracts is whether or not they are found in nature or are human-made. For our purposes, we trace the social contract discussion back to the Western Enlightenment, where it was studied and expanded on by Thomas Hobbes in his book Leviathan. Hobbes believed that life would be "solitary, poor, nasty, brutish and short without a social contract between humans."

Hobbes' description of a society with no social contract points to the commandments of the Order. Because any society that is unable or refuses to meet the requirements of the distressed is a community whose social contract is failing, and this condition is where Odd Fellows can be of help.

You are a part of one universal community, having come from the hand of a shared creative universe. You should not, therefore, become wrapped up in self and refuse to help society. Without society, what would you be? No human can be independent; man can't live on bread alone. No human can achieve greatness without the social and economic structure provided by others.

In a social organization for mutual relief, people of all classes and conditions enter into a social compact to support, protect, defend, and advise and counsel each other. Adversity will crush even the strongest, wealthiest, and most prosperous human or society. For this reason, we need organizations like the Independent Order of Odd Fellows.

Under the influence of Friendship, Love, and Truth, all the tribes and kindreds of the earth can meet and concentrate their energies for society's good. Friendship, Love, and Truth allows all nations, tongues, and creeds to understand the motive for universal fraternity. Universal fraternity is our corner-stone. On its stable base rests our superstructure. It teaches us to regard all humanity as our kin, children of a creative universe that is the author of our existence, in which we move and have our being.

8. KNOWING AND OBSERVING YOUR THOUGHTS

Odd Fellows encourage you to spend time getting to know yourself. "Do unto others as you would have them do unto you" is a statement based on knowledge of yourself. Because if you don't know yourself, how can you know others?

The outside world is full of destitution and division, but an Odd Fellow's mind must not be so. These two ideas: friendship and love, must assert their dominance over you. You must have faith in yourself and offer yourself charity and sympathy when life's decisions and events may harm you. You are a captive of your thoughts and emotions. Observe and watch them, and in this way, you can control them.

Through gloomy thoughts, emotions, and negative stories you tell yourself, you can bring yourself into a state of bondage more bitter than any human subjugation. Evil spirits, interpreted as evil thoughts, attacked King Saul and endlessly tormented him.

It would be best if you came to see any upsetting thoughts and pessimistic stories you tell yourself as a crime committed against the self. If you allow yourself to be held captive by negative stories you tell yourself and the emotions they foster, they will drag you to the lowest depths of wretchedness, misery, and despair. If you're under the control of fiery and irritable thinking, you must free yourself from their grasp by becoming the Outer Guardian of your mind and refuse them entrance. Study the role of the lodge Outer Guardian. Then develop a plan to prevent these bleak, dreary, funereal stories from gaining control of your life. Enraged and tempestuous thinking leads to undisciplined emotions that will increase the chain's shackles around you to the point where they become tighter and more challenging to break.

These thoughts and stories you tell yourself lead you to think that something will always go wrong, or you may think of your "imperfections" or that no one loves you. You may overthink when criticized, or how "worthless" you are because you compare yourself to others.

These types of thoughts will cause you to miss out on many opportunities in life. You may be afraid of going on trips, meeting people, furthering your education, or looking for better employment. They create a harassing anxiety that keeps you self absorbed, so you miss experiencing the natural and social world around you.

Damaging thoughts emphasize and magnify damage to your physical health. Presumably, if you eat spoiled food and discover it makes you ill, you'll stop eating it. Yet, even though grim thinking damages your physical health, you continue to shovel spoiled thinking into yourself by the spadeful. It is ridiculous to do this. Feeling angry or sad is a warning that you have made a petulant thought a part of you. Heed the warning and remove the idea. Is your body tense, in pain, or agitated? Are your hands grasped in a fist? Are you frowning? If so, take the time to compose yourself, then review what you have been thinking. Your body can tell you much about your mental state.

It would help if you made statements to yourself to motivate your mind and body. These statements must be believable to you and not wishful statements. The difference is between this faulty thought: "I have always made perfect decisions," and the more believable idea: "I am a good person, and I've made some pretty good decisions in my life." Or this inadequate thought: "I always do better than the next fellow because I'm the best in the world" versus a more believable: "I usually do pretty well in these situations, I just need to consider it thoroughly." Always make these motivating thoughts believable to yourself.

Decide if your thought is one of guilt, embarrassment, hatred, or insulting, then label it. Next, turn loose of it by saying, "Will it matter in five years?" If in five years the situation won't matter, decide not to care about the thought further. Remember: decide. Try not to force yourself to believe it because that rarely works. There are other ways of accomplishing this outcome, and conducting further research on your part can prove fruitful. The change in thinking comes gradually.

Identify what circumstances, situations, or people encourage your negative ideas and thinking. Once you identify these, you must move away from these people and ideas. You may need to do so gradually or all at once. Don't spend too much time trying to change other people's negative attitudes for your benefit, as this rarely works.

You may create distorted stories in your mind about another person. Be careful of misreading a person's intentions. Misreading a circumstance will produce adverse reactions in you. If you haven't heard from a friend for a while, perhaps it is because they are busy, not because they think ill of you. Be careful not to apply these distorted perspectives to another person. Communication with people is the key to avoiding this.

Here are two thought experiments. In your mind's eye, picture in detail a white circle on a black background. Hold it there as long as you can, then stop. Next, ask yourself, "Am I a white circle?" Of course, you aren't. But the white circle IS a thought, just like every other thought you have. Negative thoughts and stories are no more who you are than the white circle is. You witness the circle because you are aware of it, but you aren't a white circle. A negative thought you have may imply you're an idiot; however, you're no more an idiot than a white circle. If the stories you tell yourself do not nourish you, spit them out.

Next, picture the white circle once more, then change it into a blue square and see it with as much detail as you can. Replacing the white circle with a blue square illustrates how you can change one thought into another, and in the same way, you can change gloomy thoughts into better ones that benefit you rather than agonize you.

Your thoughts don't cause unhappiness. It's holding on to them that does. It's when you latch on to a bad idea, focus on it, and single it out that causes you unhappiness and discomfort. Mental upset is a natural alarm that notifies you that you have given a disturbing thought your riveted attention, and you're keeping it at the front of your mind.

Controlling these thoughts takes repetition. It's done the same way an animal is trained. If you let the brain run wild all day as an animal, it will ruminate on negative thoughts more and more. Train your brain to focus more often on what you're doing in the here and now, in the present, in this very instant, rather than letting it wander about "off leash." Train it over and over.

If you cannot control your thoughts and emotions, or depression and melancholy, you might need to speak to someone qualified to help professionally.

9. COMING TO KNOW YOURSELF

Your atoms have been inside of stars and floated suspended in outer space for longer than our species has existed. Most of the atoms in your body are 13.7 billion years old. Who you are is just the latest page in the incredible story of their existence. They've washed through the chemical cycles of the Earth countless times, which might have included being frozen to the top of a mountain in one eon to roaming through dense jungles as part of the thigh bone of a tyrannosaurus in the next.

We can use modern science to see the story of us from its real beginning. If you were to do this, you would discover that you are born from the universe, in the same way a wave emerges from an ocean. We don't come into the universe from somewhere else. We blossom from it like a rose from its stem.

Atoms are the minuscule building blocks of everything you see around you, including you. They make up the cells that make up your body. Although cells have a lifespan of a few days to a few years, most atoms will coast around the universe for billions and billions of years before they break down. They are practically immortal.

Knowing yourself is knowing about the science of the universe. It is also about knowing your inner self, for that which is within you reflects on the outside.

You are groping your way through life in doubt. Your reasoning and moral nature may be dark until you gain knowledge of yourself. By this, you discover your duty to society and your destiny. When the light of self-knowledge breaks on you, you will see the path you're required to tread.

Less inner hostility, enhanced decisiveness, self-control, resistance to social pressure, tolerance and understanding of others, and more pleasure in life emerge from knowing yourself more thoroughly. Knowledge about yourself is also understanding that you can use self-knowledge differently in diverse situations. Self-knowledge isn't a one-time discovery-- it's a process, and it's not unlike walking the Jericho Road.

As a child, you lived in a small bubble and tended to ignore everything but the most severe impacts on your consciousness. Society trained you to focus on the material universe and examine it, rather than analyze yourself. Hence, it's no wonder we ignore our inner selves. But if you investigate that which is outside of you, you must also examine that which is within you and apply the lesson you learn from one to the other. To know yourself more thoroughly, you must explore your values, interests, temperament, strengths, personal goals, routine activities, and life goals. It would help if you also examined your thoughts about these things.

Values like assisting others, being productive, having good health, or financial stability will guide decision making.

They can motivate you to meet your aims and ambitions. Think about your values so you'll make reputable decisions. Taking action based on your values can also keep you motivated when you feel all is lost.

Interests are things you are passionate about, like personal leisure activities or doing something for the Order. Direct your attention to anything that draws and holds your interest for an extended period. What gets your attention? What makes you curious? What concerns you?

Temperament describes your inborn preferences. Are you introverted and prefer time alone? Are you extroverted and like to be with others? Are you both? Are you a planner or prefer to float along on the stream? Do you make decisions based on how you feel or based on facts? Do you like details or big ideas?

Routine Activities refers to your daily routines. At what time of day does your energy peak? When are you sleepiest? Do you prefer late nights or mornings? When do you feel the most creative? When do you choose to conduct business during the day, and does that correspond to when others conduct business? When is a good time for you to think about new ideas? When do you prefer to start a new undertaking? Analyze your daily routines carefully to better plan your activities to fit your body, mood, and mind.

Meaningful Goals are about asking yourself, "What have been the most meaningful events of my life?" Think back, and create an inventory of them. This list, along with the other insights, can help you discover clues to your hidden identity or career.

Strengths are your abilities, skills, and talents. But also

include strengths like loyalty, respect, fairness, or love of learning. Knowing your strengths is key to self-confidence, and not understanding them can lead you into a wretched life of low self-esteem.

What are your beliefs, and do you believe them? You may think it an odd question, but your beliefs are frequently not in line with your thoughts. For instance, you might believe, as most do, that it's best to treat people nicely. Yet throughout the day, you may harbor the most horrific thoughts about people when they bother you in some way, don't agree with your political views, or believe differently. Those thoughts come from a core belief based deep inside your subconscious, and they limit your growth. You may have chosen these beliefs outright, or you may have absorbed them from acquaintances or the society in which you live. Please take steps to help yourself move beyond these defeating core beliefs.

Other questions to ask to know yourself: If something is forbidden, do you want it less or more? Are you comfortable or uncomfortable in a disorderly environment? Do you find it easier to do things for others than to do something for yourself? Is your life "on hold" in some way like until you get married, finish school, or lose weight? What people or activities give you energy or make you feel depleted?

Is there an area of your life where you feel out of control or especially in control? Dealing with out of control thoughts to guide you toward knowing yourself is a long road. You'll need to measure your progress in weeks and months, not days.

Odd Fellows are aware that some members suffer from medical situations that cause certain issues with one's thinking. If you can't benefit from changing your views or speaking with another Odd Fellow about your problems, seek counseling or medical advice.

10. THE COMBINATION OF WEALTH AND POWER

The objects which often excite our ambitions are insignificant when one watches sand move through an hourglass. Is a quest for wealth and power more important than receiving love? More important than giving love? More essential than wiping the tears of disappointment from the face of a child? The person who reflects on these examples should conclude that wealth and power and the desire for them often come at the loss of a life filled with love.

Wealth and power, when combined, are unstable. Singularly, wealth or power can be manageable, but when united, they may make you selfish and increase your sense of entitlement, even though you have done nothing special. Because wealth and power can be intoxicating, you can become addicted to their accumulation and ignore the plight of your own family, community, state, or nation. Wealth and power might make you insensitive to other people's problems, emotions, and suffering.

They can make you overconfident in your talents resulting in poor decision making.

Further, there will always be people who seek to take them from you. Some people will invariably undermine you, creating anger and frustration in your mind, leading to dysfunction in your life. Finally, when you have power and wealth, many people will despise you, which leads to instability in social relations.

Wealth and power can make those who have it unstable. Evil spirits consumed King Saul precisely because he wanted to maintain his affluence and authority. Under these spirits' influence, Saul attempted to kill his child, Jonathan, after Jonathan's friend David became as famous and influential as Saul. Are the united forces of wealth and power worth that?

Today you may be the idol of the people, flattered, honored, extolled, and crowned by them. They gather around you and intoxicate you with their applause. You are the leader of the people, the great ruler of today, but who can tell how long you will rule and be adored? An unfortunate speech, an error of conduct, a moment of indecision, and a failure to appeal to the human race's dangerous instincts will ruthlessly deprive you of your honor and glory. The idols of yesterday are today's broken statues; yesterday's heroes and heroines are the "have-beens" of today. Society's whims are erratic, short-lived, mutable, unpredictable, and impermanent.

And as the mighty fall, so the obscure rise. Names that were unknown ten years ago are blazoned almost on the skies. The insignificant come up and take the scepter in their hand. The poor street urchins of a little while ago are the wealthy merchants or the successful lawyers of today, and this becomes their hour. Their power controls the moment. Strange, is it not?

Society and civilization are always evolving. Their elements continually pass from pole to pole, from one extreme to another, while many have absorbing thoughts about how to acquire great possessions in the world. In this state of things, it's not surprising that there should be a lamentable carelessness respecting others' wants. Consequently, many deserving of a better fate are left to pine in desperate need and die unattended and unwept. It isn't strange then that those who are reduced to poverty, and galled by what they call the wrongs of the world done to them, should become a society's enemies. Adopting those means of survival, which need often encourages, they consider a just retaliation on those who they conceive have wronged them.

In such a state of uncertainty, few can leave their homes for safer places without just apprehension for their safety. Any order of things that can contribute to allay these apprehensions and lessen these uncertainties is humane. But an Odd Fellow can surf on this troubled wave of human life, and let it bear us where it may, as we have few apprehensions of want or suffering.

11. INFLUENCE

Many people make the mistake of depending on the influence of power and wealth to obtain employment and profit. This approach is a grievous drawback even if you have the talent necessary for advancement. Others will say that your success, or partial success, was due to influence rather than integrity and worthiness. Depend on your own merits. The person who depends on the influence of power and wealth faces disadvantages from the start.

Every person wins their own success. Even when the wisdom and resources of good parents and teachers attempt to direct you, you must decide whether you'll accept their aid and to what extent. You must appropriate these resources by using your intelligence and reduce them to the service of your purpose.

Parents can do a lot for their children, but they can't decide their life calling and cannot succeed for them as Saul attempted to do for Jonathan. A mother or father may get a work position for their child but can't fill it for them. Parents might win favor and respect for their children, but they can't secure it for them.

It's far better to follow the path of kindness, love, and hope than to chase the *ignis fatuus* of wealth and power. These things are perishable; they elude your grasp because one can never grasp them--they are intangible thought phantoms based on ever-changing social and personal interpretations. One doesn't die being full of wealth or full of power. But you can die being full of love. Wealth won't save you. Power cannot rescue you. Only love can comfort and ease you toward a peaceful and loving finish.

12. HEART AND HAND

As an Odd Fellow, remember that the universe reacts to what you do. Some scientists believe, and even ancient people thought that the universe is conscious and reacts to what we say, how we act, and what we believe. Its eye is always on us; it beholds and responds to the evil and the good.

The four commandments of the Order direct our focus in our communities. What your hands find to do in these respects, you should do happily with the whole heart, not grudgingly or unwillingly. True friendship goes with speed to render help when it's required. The heart and hand should go forth to alleviate the suffering of society. The emblem of the heart and hand illustrates this.

The heart and mind affected by pure Friendship, Love, and Truth will soon understand the emblem of the hand and heart. For the heart is the noble seat of our desires, and the hand must obey with action whenever such a noble soul commands; so will the hand be stretched out to an Odd Fellow in distress, not knowing how soon the same fate may be yours.

The heart in hand emblem reflects the three concepts of interest, desire, and action.

First, interest comes before the desire to accomplish something. Once you direct your interest toward an object or idea, something happens: the forces of attraction or repulsion are activated. If you find the item or idea intriguing, it will attract you. If not, the action of repulsion is triggered, and you will redirect your attention to another idea or object. Attraction to an object or idea will create a desire to act on it. So interest creates desire or the heart to help others.

The desire to help others must not be confused with forcing something to occur because you wish it. In Odd Fellowship, the desire to help others is selfless and benefits others as well as yourself. Forcing your "will" on others simply because you demand something brings only negative results.

A society or a single person cannot force their will on all of creation. This approach results in chaotic and hateful conditions, war and civil strife being two extreme examples. On a personal level, it leads to arguments and physical altercations. The person who approaches life this way is usually arrogant and overbearing and has no respect for anyone but themselves.

There is one thing to ask about a person attempting to force their will on others: "Is the person trying to help but doesn't understand how to go about it?" If this is the case, you should try and communicate with the person and explain how their approach is damaging their cause.

As an Odd Fellow, use your heart's desire as a way to be humble. You are part of a whole of humanity, not separate from it, not better than it; in the lodge, we're all the same. Working with humility will guide you in learning how the universe works and how to work with it and use it to help society and nature.

Without desire and setting goals, humans would accomplish nothing. The desire to build, create, think, and examine are examples. Imagine a universe without desire, without "the heart to help others." Without desire, you wouldn't experience a full life or have any moral or mental growth, and nothing would evolve. So, having the heart to do something is the same as having the desire to do it. The notion of having a heart is an illustration of having the desire to accomplish a task. You must have the heart to serve others.

The heart is the part of the human body that is the fountain of life and the most marvelous in its motions. When all other members of your body are at rest, the heart is in perpetual motion from the first to the last moment of your life. If you ask someone to point to themselves, they most likely will point to their heart. Since it's the mystical seat of our emotions and affections, penetrate your heart with love and respect to all that we are bound to by solemn obligation.

Once the desire has arisen, the hand supplies the action to accomplish the goal. Taking action is the result of interest and desire. Action is the physical act of reaching toward your goal. It is what you do in the physical realm that leads to results.

The hand represents an action; because of all the parts of the human body, the hand is the most active. By our hands, we indicate our thoughts when our words can't be understood; by using our hands, we have a universal language, and with the hand, we describe and point out all circumstances of time, place, and manner of what we relate. With the hand, we express the heart's affection, soothe discomfort, approve or disapprove, permit or prohibit, admire or manifest our contempt, so that by the action of our hands, our enemies and friends may, in many cases, understand our meaning in the dark as easily as at noonday.

The rose, mentioned in our degree work, is like the heart and is a symbol of desire or want. Alchemists used the emblem of links of roses to represent desires and goals in alchemy. Transmute these vines into links of the purest gold by excluding all thoughts and actions that are incompatible with your primary purpose. If you do this, you can achieve remarkable things. Each link represents a process, and if you focus on Friendship, Love, and Truth, the results can change minds and communities.

Links of roses can tell you much. Use Friendship to make you wholly acquainted with your goal. Collect the facts. Make your goal your new friend and find out all you can about it. Love your goal. Appreciate it, support it, feed it, take care of it. Make your goal your child to raise. Make sure over and over the facts about your plan are true. Then apply Truth in the actions directed toward your goal so that you know the actions you take are delivered truthfully and with a definite effect. Is it true that each decision or action you take is the best one based on your research?

The rose is seen in its beauty as it spreads its leaves to the morning sun. It will also die, losing its grace and form, its leaves scattered on the ground so no one can gather them. The spoiler is among your works, as it should be, for all things--including interest, desire, and action--bloom then fade away.

13. TRANSFORMING YOUR FUTURE AS AN ODD FELLOW

"Dust thou art, and to dust thou shalt return."

You'll find this assertion in most mystical writings throughout human history. There is a predictable cycle of things, a beginning, a middle, and an end--*and a beginning again-- but differently*. It means that change is a law of the universe. It's easily observable that all things change, and all things end. That there is a rising and falling. An Odd Fellow must learn to accept change and work with it to your advantage.

The universe wants you to grow. It's structured to force growth through change, even among the most stubborn humans. You'll know you are changing when you suddenly begin to see things differently. You might see friendships through a different lens, view your job differently, or have a new realization about a particular situation. These are signals to an Odd Fellow that they have changed within themselves. Learn to recognize these changes in you because they tell you much about your inner self.

46

You may know people who seem to have never changed. They have remained in their little cocoons of safety as best they can. They are usually a bore to speak with, and you might be amazed at how they seem stuck in time. But the universe, even in these situations, pushes people to learn.

Change is one way we learn. We change jobs, learn new things, or change our opinions when we hear others' views. We base our education on change, for we can learn nothing unless we replace our old way of thinking. The universe pushes us to learn, and the curriculum is transformation.

Although you are under the control of the universe and its innovations, you can also participate with it. Each day of your life, you have the opportunity to work along with the universe and alter yourself and your surroundings to create a better experience. You may wish to change your diet, change jobs, change hairstyles, or change how you think about your life. So, as the universe transforms around you, there is the opportunity for you to change along with it for the better. When the universe changes around you and things become different, try and choose an innovation for yourself that will lead to better results.

Odd Fellowship seeks to improve and elevate the character of humankind. To transform ourselves and civilization, we have an essential tool: our hopes and dreams for the future. Every society has ambitions. Every person has ambitions, young and old alike, with no exception. It's automatic. We'd have no prospects if we didn't dream or imagine what our futures will be. Without memory, constructing a future would be difficult.

47

Memory presides over the past and deals with things that have been. Imagination presides over the future and the unseen. Imagination constructs things that are to be, while memory brings in the actual and known. When you hear of a person you have never seen, you instinctively make an image of them in your mind. When you read of a place you've never seen, you attempt to create a picture of it in your mind's eye. When you hear of an event described by another, you try to imagine what it was like. When you think of your future, you try and create an image of what you would like it to be.

Understand that the way you imagine your future is a direct reflection of who you are at that moment. The same is for a community or lodge: whatever it imagines for its future reflects its present moment. Things you want to purchase, trips you want to take, or hobbies you wish to start are reflections of the moment in which they are imagined. If your image of the future is chaotic, stop and look around.

Does chaos in your current life surround you? If so, make changes to make things better. Can you imagine a better future for you and society while things are chaotic around you? If so, this is the proper direction, and the only thing left to do is find the resources you need to get yourself to your imagined future. Your dreams and imagination reflect your present character and indicate what you'll become.

The universe allows you to use the ambitions you have for your future to co-create with it--to change or transform yourself, your lodge, and community into something better. Your imagination is the higher half-shadow of reality. When you cease to paint pictures of your future, the Odd Fellow should reflect on the lessons of the Initiatory Degree.

To improve your future, you must paint a picture of it in your mind's eye that's completely accurate down to the exact colors and dimensions. Once you do this, create a plan to reach what your imagination has created. Don't imagine a situation where you attempt to control another person's future because this will violate the dictates of Friendship, Love, and Truth. If you can't form pictures in your mind, you should write about it to make it as real as possible on paper.

A key to creating a future for your lodge, community, or yourself is to imagine the day after your goal is fulfilled. Think about what the day after would be like.

As a person furnishes their own home, flat, or apartment until it becomes an externalization of their own ideals and qualities in the outer environment, so we all form inner environments and fashion the inner world in which we live. Better days are coming because we dream of them.

One's dreams and imagination individualize and, at the same time, socialize us. They are the reality out of which the actual comes. The life that has its roots in the unseen idea is the only life that bears its fruits in the seen and tangible. However, you must struggle to bring the image to fruition. This struggle is the equivalent of fire's effect on the alchemist's chemicals.

Remove the chains, Odd Fellow, and follow your dreams responsibly.

14. CYCLES IN NATURE

The universe has cycles it goes through.

When you begin to look at the universal cycle, realize this: that to survive, to operate continually, the universe is designed to create, build up, then break itself down innumerable times a second so it can be reborn and start again. The universe is designed to regenerate itself. This process calls to mind the wisdom of the serpent, which sheds its skin and regenerates itself. The Ouroboros, the serpent that devours its tail, illustrates this idea.

The Ouroborus eats itself, yet it still lives. The Ouroboros is in the shape of a circle and helps explain life cycles and the beginning and end of things. We also see the circle or spiral used in many rituals. The serpent that winds its way around a walking stick is a reminder of this and represents humanity's continued evolution toward universal brother and sisterhood. The serpent may be the symbol of life throwing off the past and continuing to live.

You live by consuming something that was recently alive, whether plant or animal, and all things consume other things to sustain their lives just as the universe does. The universe survives by destroying and consuming itself so it can be reborn and continue to exist. Things on earth break down, and what remains is used by other life forms to survive.

Besides the serpent eating its tail, another symbol that illustrates this universal cycle is the moon, an emblem still used by the Rebeckahs. It goes through its cycles of the dark of the moon, to the waxing crescent, to the full moon, to a waning crescent, to the dark of the moon, then to waxing crescent again. The moon's cycle is mentioned in Jonathan and David's story when Saul celebrates the New Moon Feast. In those days, the New Moon was the evening of the first waxing crescent after the dark of the moon. Some say this point in the story coincides with the rise of David to become king.

The sun also goes through its cycles as it progresses through the sky daily. Beginning in the east, it reaches its triangular apex at noon, then travels to the west until finally darkness arrives. The sun's daily path illustrates Friendship, Love, and Truth as shown on a triangle used on some of the Order's regalia.

In some early lodges, the Vice Grand represented the emblem of the moon. This is perhaps one reason the Vice Grand wears the color blue or blue sash. In some mystic rites, the moon represented the subconscious, and the sun illustrated the outer or objective world since it made the world visible. In some early Odd Fellows lodges, the Noble Grand was dressed in red or wore a red sash, and represented the sun.

Another symbol of the cycles are the solstices and equinoxes. Before the winter solstice, the days are short in the northern hemisphere, darkness is prevalent as sunlight is scarce. On the day of the winter solstice, the days begin to lengthen again, bringing more light to the northern hemisphere but less light to the southern hemisphere, where the days become shorter. The example of these two hemispheres also illustrates the balance of nature between cycles, and one can see this represented by the balance scale as one side goes up and the other down; we see it in ritual when a candidate is brought from darkness to light.

The tides of the ocean ebb and flow, and in their cycle, they do both twice in twenty-four hours. The mariner who misses a floodtide doesn't abandon his voyage; nor does he deliberately sail into the "shallows" nor indulge in "miseries." He watches for the next flood. The tide in the affairs of society also ebbs and flows many times during the average lifetime. If there is an analogy here, it is that of hope. This example teaches that if you're inexperienced in worldly ways, the next tide is equally available if you miss the first flood tide.

Society has cycles that it follows. For instance, the holidays, birthdays, weekends, and the four seasons affect how a community cyclically reacts and conducts itself. For example, Friday afternoons are probably a terrible day to contact a bank to discuss business. Monday mornings are probably a poor choice for holding meetings. The winter holidays may be a difficult time for shopping. Conduct your research in these matters and apply them.

Your life follows the same cycle of change. Life is a vapor that appears for a little time and then vanishes away. Where are the infinite members of the human family who lived and figured on the earth? They sleep with their fathers, and the places that once knew them well will know them no more forever. You should seriously meditate and reflect on this knowledge of what you are soon to be and what you might become.

Realize when things are at their best, in their season, and know how to appreciate and take advantage of them. The works of nature all climb to a peak of perfection: up to it they wax and beyond it they wane. It's the mark of elegance and taste to enjoy everything at its best, although many may not know how.

15. CREATING, PRODUCING and WORKING

An industrious Odd Fellow seldom suffers the agony of want. True, sometimes circumstances beyond your control can make you financially, mentally, or socially poor or troubled. Even though your labors may only yield you a little, you must tell yourself that it's good that you're attempting to provide for yourself and those who need you. No person can be happy without creating and working. The universe wouldn't exist if it weren't always creating and laboring, and so it is with you. The person who chooses idleness is an unhappy person who drags out a miserable existence. Simultaneously, the laborer's sleep is sweet and refreshing; that of the idler is restless, unsatisfying, and given to scheming.

Most people are unhappy if they aren't producing, creating, and contributing. The mighty strength of the universe concentrates on building up and breaking down by designing and producing--even the universe labors-- and so must you. Again, there are times where it might be out of your control that you're not employed. Even so, create or produce as best you can. As a member of this Order, you must labor, if not for yourself, for society and the advancement of civilization.

Through fields of toil--sowing, watering, plowing, and reaping--you'll hasten toward your goals. Not creating and working can destroy a mind. The farmer, unskilled laborer, mechanic, artist, writer, salesman, clerk, minister, thinker, poet, philosopher are all workers if they *are earnest* in their calling. Humanity in us dies when we begin to accept ease instead of growth or pleasure instead of truth.

Gifts require payment of some kind. As "freely" supplied by the universe, the gifts of light, air, and water must still be worked for. You must strive to open your eyes. Lungs must be moved, and the lips must be parted and moved. No one is ever successful without hard labor and working smartly in his calling. Labor and production show your respect for the worth of life, that you are willing to toil for its high ends. Labor has emancipated, educated, developed, and interpreted the human spirit. It has made humanity acquainted with itself. It has set us in harmony with nature. Through self-control, character, moral power, and educational influence, we've created civilization.

Creating things, producing, and working is a means of happiness. We often find that some of the most miserable people don't build, make, or work in any fashion. When this happens, they often "get inside their head" and begin to focus on destructive thoughts and ideas. Not creating can be worse than overworking in some cases.

Evil has many opportunities at an idle person, and unproductive people grow cynical, angry, and unjust. They will become selfish, unfraternal, and unsympathetic. Unproductive people can also form dangerous underclasses in societies. This is why a community must create a structure that allows all community members to be successful.

16. THRIFT

Thrift implies frugality, economy, good management, prudence, carefulness. We should say it means these things in all the walks of life,—regarding business, social, intellectual and religious life, and personal care.

First, regarding business life: Can a young Odd Fellow starting out in the world ever hope to gain a foothold, firm, and sure, without constant practice of frugality? Those who thoughtlessly, carelessly, or willfully spend all their earnings are creating for themselves a time of poverty, want, and despair, a time when you'll see loved ones suffer for the things you can't provide. To spend all you make week in and week out, and perhaps a little more borrowed from a friend, you mean well and fully intend paying back what you borrowed, but living expenses increase. Maybe illness throws you out of work for a time. Then you're forced to borrow more to tide you over to better days.

Debts have a fantastic way of increasing and fastening themselves around a person's neck like a great rock. You can become so burdened with debt you cannot put forward your best energies; your sleep is troubled and broken, and your earning capacity declines.

You may see many opportunities where you could make a comfortable living. You feel you could do so if you were only out of debt and had just a little to start with. You struggle hard and might, with many sacrifices, be able to pay off your just and honest debts. But, your golden opportunities have passed you by. And, your ambition and strength of the body may begin to fail you because of overwork and stress.

Or suppose you can't pay off your debts, and illness, loss of position, or many other misfortunes overtake you. In that case, you may die, leaving a heritage of obligations. You leave a clouded name to those who loved you and had a right to look to you for support. Your loved ones may know in their soul that you were honest and meant well. Still, many would believe you dishonest, thriftless, and shiftless. All because you didn't know how or couldn't see the necessity of taking care of the pennies and living within your income.

In contrast to this, we will take someone of the same age with less ability and much smaller earnings. They look around them and see those who have made a success in life and those who have failed. Those who have started with only their energy and determination to aid them have made great fortunes, beginning with a mere pittance for wages or salary. They think the matter over and compare the lives of those around them. They soon conclude—'Tis not what a person makes, but what they save, that totals their real worth.

They see people next to them earning far more than them, yet those earner's motto is live while you live, and they spend it as fast as they make it. So they determine within themselves to practice thrift, live within what they make, and save a little besides. This they do faithfully and systematically, and in a few years, an opportunity to wisely invest their savings presents itself. Soon they find themselves climbing more easily each successive round of the ladder of financial success.

Thrift affects your moral and intellectual life, as well as your social life. Socially—by providing society with better surroundings, better homes, better clothes, etc. Intellectually— by giving you more time and more money to devote to study, self-culture, art, literature, travel—all that pertains to culture and refinement. Morally—by giving you the means not only to be useful but to do good.

The frugal person practices self-denial by doing without some things they think are almost necessary. They might curb their appetite. Or, develop the determination to give up some longed-for pleasure. But all such denials repay many fold by giving great strength of character and the power to conquer oneself. When a person masters themselves, then they can rule others.

Thrift regarding physical life will not permit one to waste their strength or use up their energies by frivolous time use. It teaches that they must have proper recreation, proper food, and adequate rest. Thrift teaches you to become a master of self instead of a slave to personal desires. It teaches holding your physical being in subjection to your better self-- the economy of strength, economy of time, and the economy of earnings.

To practice thrift, avoid the little leaks—the spending of little driblets here and there. Save the pennies, the nickels, the dimes, and succeed you must and will. Have more than one income, always. Be as thrifty as the bee, laying by in the summertime of youth for the winter of old age.

Don't mistake the notion of thrift for a miserliness or stinginess. These two issues have their own problems and must be guarded against.

17. ACTS OF CHARITY

However flawed or despised you think you are, you're never entirely friendless. Humanity's natural kindness for those who need help can't die. If you are forsaken, at the very least, sympathy for your trouble will arrive. Don't resist this help, but return it.

Sometimes, in some people, kindness becomes blunted. Their heart is hardened, and they lose the ability to regard the sorrows of the distressed. The purpose of organizations like Odd Fellows is to help banish selfishness and keep alive the desire to aid and care for others by encouraging people in social and humane duties. As Odd Fellows, our work is a constant battle with selfishness.

An act of charity creates a luster around the donor. It establishes a crown of glory to the meek and merciful of heart who give to others. It challenges other people to live up to your standards--it even prompts contests of giving by others.

Generosity is not just a word; it's a deed. "Blessed are the merciful, for they shall obtain mercy." Charity will teach you about the lives of the suffering, how to locate them, how to help them, and how to protect them because it's your duty as an Odd Fellow to do so.

An Odd Fellow's charity springs from the heart. It softens your emotions and will please you. The poor *and* rich love charity's dispenser, and kind people are honored and respected at home and abroad. You'll enjoy the relationships you build doing charitable work.

Charity isn't always about providing money to those who suffer. It could require helping someone look for work, taking them to a doctor's appointment, or taking care of their children or pet in an emergency. You can express charity in a multitude of ways.

The Odd Fellow, who is charitable, looks on the suffering world--whether human or the natural environment-- as the objects of their regard and care. As long as you have the duty to relieve suffering, you should perform the task with pleasure.

Charity's aim isn't only to alleviate misery, it also strives to prevent it. Charity is a mindset. And as such, charity keeps a watchful eye on threatening situations. It thrusts out its protecting hand to prevent danger and warn of coming danger to those who might be under threat. It smooths over society's faults and failings and tries to find the causes of those frailties rather than hold them up to the world's view to injure those affected. It understands that people are erring beings and can't avoid the failings incident to human nature.

At the very base of charity is the golden rule of doing unto others. When you practice charity and teach it to others, you'll receive honors and a more prosperous future. Admiration and caring dwell among those who meet together to relieve those who suffer. If ignited in our hearts, goodwill for each other and the world will burn brighter and brighter. If admiration, and caring dwell in you, and you lead by example, they will bring you happiness. Our Order is one where our best feelings gather around the central aim of relieving those in distress. If you follow the obligations of your relationship with the Order, you won't be controlled by selfishness or indifference.

"In union is strength," is a common adage. Consider uniting with lodge members in the cause of Odd Fellowship in your deeds and works. One person, if they focus on their work, can accomplish much in the field of charity. But a group of people united in the service of compassion can transform the world. Suppose you, along with other Odd Fellows, labor with one heart and one mind on the highways and byways of life. In that case, people will feel the influence in your community. Working together your lodge is capable of crushing, withering, and eradicating the demons of greed, wrath, and pride and raising society to a higher level of living.

Don't forget your obligations. Don't wait for others to initiate charity--do your part, though you might be one rod in a bundle.

Wherever humanity is found, in whatever situation of life, they are composed of the things that make up the entire universe. No matter how poor or degraded a person might be, there are signs of human equality. If you can do anything to promote their happiness or you can relieve their wants *without jeopardizing you or yours,* DO IT, for it's your duty.

If there's a good plan to improve their condition, engage it with all your heart's desire, remembering that those you labor for are your kin and composed of the same universal spark as you. We're all made of the same dust, and it rains on both the honest and dishonest--for the universe sees us equally as created beings. Don't stop to inquire about a sufferer's creed, faith, title, or condition, but consider that with all their errors and imperfections, they are your universal family. And so it is on the road to Jericho.

Do to others as you would like to have done to you; love your neighbor as yourself; regard all humanity as kin: all children of the universe are equal--from the monarch on a throne, to the beggars in rags--and universal love is what they require.

18. INNOCENCE

Innocence is a lovely quality that adorns human nature. The corrupt laugh at it, but in their hearts, they honor it. You will occasionally see even the most evil at heart drawn to honor and integrity. The agreeable, incorruptible, and compassionate are beloved by the most abandoned wretches that disgrace society. People respect those who are innocent regarding misconduct, and if you're innocent, the world is with you.

In our Order, we have sacred links that bind us. If there is *one* link touched by violence or corruption, the chain's golden purity is broken. So let there be no strife between you and other members, for we're all Odd Fellows. The Order professes principles that destroy the chaff and stubble of bickering and refine society's powers and faculties.

If you want the best for yourself, you must be sober, temperate, and not corruptible. This doesn't mean you shouldn't "eat, drink, and be merry." Of course, you should, if you wish. The important thing is to not overindulge. You must strive toward balance and keep an eye on the emblem of the scales unless you go too far in one direction and succumb to a wretched existence. Work as hard as possible not to bring disgrace on yourself by embracing a lifestyle without balance.

19. MUTUAL RELIEF

Mutual relief is a way of aiding one another in a time of distress, danger, or difficulty, and it's an aim of Odd Fellowship. A system of mutual relief cultivates the sympathies and relieves the woes of society. The shame of dependence on charity felt by those who receive it isn't the least of their difficulties. The pale cheek and the hollow eye may have revealed their suffering long before they receive aid.

Sometimes in secret, a person's pride will lead the sufferer to grieve and exhaust themselves with worry. At times, they are driven to crime. Often a person won't ask for help, even though the consequences of not doing so are dire. The fierceness of hunger and desire for shelter, praying on a frail nature, will cause them to commit foul deeds, which they would never have committed a short time before. A mutual relief system will prevent this crushing misery and save the victim from despair and society from crime.

If you saw a child drowning, you would jump in and save it, even if you were wearing nice clothes. Now consider the fact that children die every hour from poverty. Isn't the principle behind saving a drowning child one can see with one's own eyes, and saving an unknown child on the other side of the world the same?

There is a gap between the urgency and contribution to saving a child drowning in water and drowning in poverty. Some say they are afraid too much money will go to administrative costs and would rather keep the money in a local community, or that their act of charity will do little in the face of such an enormous difficulty. Others imply that their money is theirs and they would rather spend it on themselves.

However, it's important to point out that people who can give charity funds live in places where making money is possible. In areas where donations are needed, people do not make enough to donate to others. Millions of people can't give to the needy and may work exceedingly harder than you do to scrape together a pittance for themselves and their families.

For some people, receiving charitable donations is difficult. They can become emotional when they are the recipient of aid or if an inquiry is made regarding their situation. Numerous people have trouble asking for help and aid. As an Odd Fellow, you must be aware of the various reasons they might decline help or become emotional because of it:

Some people feel their life mission is always to help others, and when it's time for them to receive help, they are incapable of asking for it. Because they have created an identity based around helping, to ask for help would be invalidating who they are.

Some people deny that they need help and will argue against receiving it. These people could be depressed, suffering from anxiety, or some other disorder and may not be aware of it. Sometimes refusing help is a response they have created to help them through life.

They may tell themselves that even though they are suffering, they still have it easier than others. These people may have overconfidence in the "pull yourself up by your bootstraps" adage. They believe in self-reliance to the point of damaging themselves or their family. In the past, they may have asked for help and were told by others to "get over it" or "welcome to life." Rather than risk hearing that again, they avoid asking for help.

Some people don't want to be a burden on other people. Or they might think that receiving charity will make them the unwanted center of attention from others.

Keep these issues in mind when attempting to help someone. And, if they refuse your help in any way, you must back away until they can accept it. It's not the responsibility of the Order to force assistance on anyone.

20. ARRANGING CHARITY

As an archer takes pride in hitting his target, you should take pride in being sure your generous deeds are adequately done. Don't randomly do these things. Do your charitable deeds in a way that maximizes their benefit for the proper time, place, and circumstance. Remembering this could prevent the loss of goods to be delivered or delivered to the wrong place or avoid embarrassment to the recipient.

Properly planning the delivery of charity items is an integral part of what Odd Fellows do. Whether a tornado, earthquake, a child in distress, or homelessness, planning is essential to accomplishing your aim. Remember, the heart is the desire, and the hand is action, and action requires a proper procedure. Lack of direction causes a lack of motivation. A poor understanding of your charity aims will result in spending efforts in the wrong areas and wasting time and energy, and you'll probably end up doing the same work over again. Consider preparing for the interruptions that inevitably occur.

You'll need to involve the right people in the planning process. Be sure your lodge committee contains the people who will be the most competent people for the job. Be sure you communicate the planning information to *everyone*. This helps when problems arise, like when someone is sick, and someone needs to fill in. Your goals should be specific, contain benchmarks, and produce results people can see. Again, you don't want to do the same work twice. Also, lodge members must follow and understand the product of your work. Do the members of your committee find your project acceptable? If not, issues involving the completion of the project will arise. Be prepared to reward your committee members in some way for their efforts. Finally, be sure your goals and actions are realistic and fit a proper time frame.

21. FRIENDSHIP

In Odd Fellowship, there are many levels of friendship. The universe itself is friendship at work. All the laws of physics and nature work together and complement each other, which is nothing more than friendship between elements. It's as if the elements have formed their own social contract to benefit and support each other in constructing our temporal reality.

Friendship hears all things and is a step toward personal enrichment. The spirit of friendship inspires anyone that gives up their comfort and belongings to serve or save a friend. There are multitudes over the centuries who have offered their very lives for their friends. By doing so, they sacrificed much to benefit all of society. Some have fought against tyranny, some have fought against oppression, and some have fought to preserve the natural world. In all these instances, their goal was supporting and maintaining friendship.

Researchers have found that there are six different levels of friendship. Friendly acknowledgment involves short interactions that are amicable. Perhaps you greet one another pleasantly, but little more transpires. You may do this with different people several times per day. An acquaintance would be someone you talk with because you're in the same place simultaneously, but the meeting was not prearranged. When you agree to meet with a person later, but only in the setting you typically interact with, this may be the beginning of a friendship.

An evolving friendship is having both people make an effort to do things together. Or you might arrange to meet after work. Spending lots of time together often in different places means you and the other person have bonded as friends. Finally, a person you share your hopes, dreams, and secret thoughts with is a close friend.

You will need friends and acquaintances, or your affections will decline. Our intellectual and active powers increase with our attachments. Friends become a mirror to you by helping you see and learn about yourself. Every friend gained increases your enjoyment of life. Every friend's mind is soil, where we sow our ideas that become fruitful and blossom in the years to come. Our friends are often our salvation, so your dearest friends must be respectable because you grow to be like them.

If your friend has a bad reputation, you'll experience suffering. The persons you are most seen with will define you. If friends have poor reputations, you can't win the respect of merchants, lawyers, or physicians, or good citizens generally. And the same thing goes for your lodge: if your members have poor reputations, your lodge's reputation will suffer. Do not recruit people into your lodge who have many personal problems and "need a good influence in their lives." For they will only bring their problems into your lodge and destroy it. An initiate should be ready to help and support others, not ready to receive help and support from the lodge.

You may not have the same tastes as your friend, but friendship requires a couple of things: first, it requires truth so that each person knows the other may be trusted and genuine. Second, it requires kindness, which is a component of love, so that each approach one another equally.

Generally, it is best to form friendships with those on your general level, and among those who are working toward bettering themselves as you should be doing. You may also choose friends who are on a higher level than you if you have tastes in common.

But don't pursue a friendship with those who fall below the status of your ideals because this will slow your momentum of bettering yourself or completely extinguish your personal improvement. If you do befriend a person of this sort, only do so if they promise they will work themselves up to your level. If they do not, you must move on, and leaving a friendship this way creates emotional hardship. This is why you should scrutinize your friendships.

The first link in the Odd Fellow's chain is friendship. A faithful and loyal friend is a living treasure and is honorable and deeply lamented when gone. Nothing is more common than to talk about a friend; nothing more difficult than to find one; nothing more rare than to improve with a friend's advice as we must. The only reward of good character *is* a good character. The only way to have a friend is to be one. Such is friendship.

Forgiveness in friendship is a must, for everyone makes mistakes. If your friend hurts you in some way, find a way to discuss it gently and rationally. Reliability is vital in a friendship--knowing that you can call on someone for help is a great comfort. Just understand that the friend must feel the same way about you. Encourage in-depth discussions and the sharing of emotions in your friendships. Also, be aware that envy and jealousy can destroy a friendship--we learn about this in our degree work. If you are isolated from your family, use friendship to create your own family. Having friendships is a great source of happiness.

To make friends, turn to your lodge brothers and sisters. You will find that you have things in common with some more than others. But since Odd Fellowship operates in a certain way, friendships flow freely in a lodge. If you argue with another lodge member, ask another Odd Fellow, perhaps the Noble Grand, to intervene.

To make friends outside of the lodge requires action: inviting people to a meal, an event, a walk, or introducing yourself to people. You don't have to be charismatic to have friends. It's often merely about professing the good things you find in other people, so compliment them sincerely, show enthusiasm when you greet them, and ask them about their lives in a way that doesn't imply nosiness. You must also reach out to friends by checking in occasionally to see how they're doing.

If you believe a friend is having issues with depressing thoughts, tell them you care about them. It's important to let them know they are loved and that they matter to you. If you cannot express this, then with their permission, visit or sit with them, so they know you're available for them. Often depressing thoughts make people feel more alone than they've ever felt, so they must know that you stand by their side--that's what Odd Fellowship is about.

If a friend is having a difficult time, ask them what you can do to assist them. Check-in on them, offer to cook them meals, or run errands for them. Sometimes your friend might need someone to talk to, so ask them if you can be that person. If they refuse the help, respect their feelings.

Sometimes, depressing thoughts can turn into thoughts of suicide. This is dangerous territory and may not be something you can personally help with as an Odd Fellow. This situation is not about telling them to be warmed and filled and walk away, but being available to aid someone in distress. One of the first things you should do is to encourage them to see a professional medical practitioner. You should also take their threats of suicide seriously--don't think they are only doing it to seek attention because you aren't qualified to make that assumption. Don't believe they will never go through with suicide--again, you are not qualified to make that assumption.

Allow your friends some space and independence. Your friend, not matter how great they are, can't be there for you every minute, almost no one can. This would be an unhealthy dependency.

You don't need hundreds of friends. But having one or two people who are the closest to you can be more than rewarding. You should also take care of your friends and let them know you care. Also, be on the alert to the needs of your friends.

20. THE OPPRESSED

Many people have received inspiration from the universe to go forth as a leader in the oppressed's cause. Odd Fellows must go forth with the same universal authority as leaders in support of the oppressed. Under the sway of this inspiration, you can smite with power the high, thick walls of prejudice which shut humans away from one another and protect people from poverty, discrimination, sickness, war, natural calamity, and social upheaval-- enemies which would enslave and crush them.

To understand the iron hand of oppression, you must first understand something about the oppressors. Generally, those who oppress others can do so because of how a society is organized, not because a person seeks to oppress others.

Some communities might encourage oppression in a workplace, through a government, a family, or a school. A person who remains intolerant can only do so because society benefits that train of thought. Sometimes, the oppressor may not be aware they oppress others--instead they benefit from belonging to a group with significant advantages over other people.

In many places, heavy oppression seems to brood on the air, yet some may not realize this because, to them, the injustice is hidden. By masking or hiding injustice, an oppressive society keeps the public unaware it exists. Society hides oppression by trivializing it, blaming the oppressed for their own oppression, or diverting attention from it.

It's essential to supply the distressed with basic needs, and it's also crucial to recognize that the distressed are often the most downtrodden. Those who work *to support the oppressed* may be labeled as "divisive." Yet those who *are* the oppressors have created the divisiveness. The characterization of being divisive is used because helping the oppressed can make the oppressor feel uncomfortable. The oppressor uses this tactic to help them retain power.

In this state of things, it's not surprising that there is an unfortunate carelessness respecting others' basic needs. Consequently, many deserving a better fate are left to pine in want and die unattended and unwept. Others, reduced to poverty, and annoyed by the wrongs of society directed at them, will become its enemies. They will adopt depraved means of survival, including unethical behaviors, which oppression often encourages. It's not strange, then, that they will consider retaliation on those they think have oppressed them.

In such a state of uncertainty, few can seek safety in other lands without worrying about their safety. Anything that can contribute to calm these worries and lessen these uncertainties is humane. You should be a messenger of peace and goodwill, promise, and hope, which will make your own life more fulfilled, desirable, and promising. Don't be wearied in your progress. Go forward forever in the name of friendship and truth and bear ever the olive branch of peace to the oppressed.

23. GUARDING AGAINST SELFISHNESS AND ENMITY

While you should be harmless as a dove, you should also be wise as a serpent. Allow no person, even if they say they're an Odd Fellow, to deceive you by false expressions and demonstrations. All aren't Odd Fellows who take the name, and many are not the co-laborers they claim to be.

Closely observe any person if they are selfish, greedy, uncompassionate, or have anger issues. *Without putting you and yours at risk*, reform them if you can--but during the reforming process, don't take them into your confidence. Don't reveal private things to them. Revealing financial matters, family matters, work matters, and other personal things could make reliable weapons against you if wielded by such a person. Do your own work, but don't make them your partner in it. Be very cautious making a person of this type a lodge member.

Don't offer lodge membership to someone who you feel needs a positive impact in their life. Lodges need members who are *already able* to help those in need. Later, if the person you have in mind rises to the level of being ready to aid others, then offer them membership.

If someone you know never seems happy when you achieve something or becomes more competitive due to your achievement, this is a sign of envy. When envy drives a person, you should reflect on the lessons of the Degree of Friendship and Jonathan and David's story. Saul's treatment of David is a perfect example of envy and jealousy.

Envy generally involves two people, while jealousy involves three. Envy can be summed up by saying "I want what you have." You can be envious of wealth, status, or someone's good looks. Being envious of someone's status is comparing yourself to another and indicates lower self esteem on your part. Status is transitory, it always changes, so if someone has status today, they may not have it tomorrow. Many ancient teachings as well as those of Odd Fellowship caution against comparing yourself to others. If you feel envious, recognize it, then think of your own struggles. The person you perceive as high status is not capable of walking your road--they would not be strong enough to stand it.

If someone is dismissive of your hobbies and dreams, this is a person you might wish to avoid.

Anyone who attempts to steal your work to get the same recognition does not care about ethics or morality. They will do whatever it takes to take the easy way out.

If someone prefers to wallow in self-pity instead of helping themselves, this person is someone you should be careful around to keep that behavior from rubbing off on you. These people play the victim but never take responsibility *for what they are personally capable of fixing,* and think only of themselves. Yet, some issues like sickness, mental illness, family problems, financial problems, or oppression by society and governments may be beyond a person's control. Often these things cannot be fixed by a single person but require the work of a community. In these cases, compassion for the person is necessary.

Those who criticize others but don't know how to apply criticism to themselves are hypocritical. They speak against others repeatedly because that's easier than solving their own problems. They attack others to help build themselves up in front of others.

Odd Fellowship is ever at battle against selfishness. The selfishness of our society needs correcting. How many innovative and creative spirits have been dampened by the world's selfishness? How many bold desires? How many inventions and discoveries that could benefit society have been discouraged? How much pessimism and ruin produced? It's expected for Odd Fellows to encourage creative energies and overcome selfishness.

To encourage a generous spirit of kindness--to become more sympathetic and rid society of selfishness--is one of the noblest missions in which you can engage. A person who would place an obstruction in the way of eliminating selfishness has not learned the lessons of friendship and love. Those who are bound by the chains of bigotry and arrogance have desires that are cold and indifferent and will not bind up the wounds of a stranger or give shelter to the outcast unless the sufferer surrenders to the beliefs of the stubborn and rigid "helper." Be cautious taking help from someone who demands you believe what they believe.

Stubborn and rigid people are stuck in their ideas and assumptions, and they believe themselves to be correct in all their beliefs, rather than ask the critical questions about why they believe these things. As an Odd Fellow, *you must always be in search of truth*. In *truth is found authenticity*. You must question your own assumptions and beliefs as much as you might question others, and you must do this daily. If not, you may come to believe things that are no longer true, which might cause hurt to others. Or, you might think something which was never true to begin with, which to others can make you seem delusional.

The old saying "you can't judge a book by its cover" applies not just to people. It must also apply to beliefs and ideas which persons or societies say are true. Because you can't judge an idea by its "cover" any more than you can a person-- ideas also wear masks. You must watch any idea you get from another carefully and check with others regarding its viability.

Is the idea reasonable? Are the arguments supported by educated and recognized authorities and experts in their field, or are they rumors and lies spread by unqualified persons who seek fame, wealth, and power? Where did you first hear it?

Why is the idea important? Can it do harm? If so, to whom? Why should you believe it? What proof is there in support of the idea? You should also examine an idea through different lenses: How would a person of the opposite gender, different skin color, other religion, different geographical location, or education level view it?

24. TRUTH

An Odd Fellow should always test the waters of truth. We need to be philosophers of truth and not just assume that truth in Odd Fellowship means only "to tell the truth." Truth is much deeper, more sublime, quick to judge, and quick to liberate. To be a better Odd Fellow, you must become a better thinker. Truth is what we must strive for in all our investigations throughout our lives. It is a reward for asking pertinent questions about life. In truth, we find stability, equality, justice, and high ethical standards.

Know this: Truth is more important than your desire to be correct.

Often people become personally attached to an idea to the point that they argue as if their opinion is an extension of themselves and as if they will be physically or mentally damaged if their belief is incorrect. They will argue past what's reasonable and reject and ignore even the best evidence against it. A disagreement over an idea becomes a battleground for them, one where "losing" isn't acceptable under any circumstances. It is impossible to learn or change your views or grow and enrich your life when you think about winning or losing the discussion of an idea you believe to be true.

There are many ways to view truth. One type of truth is a reflection of reality. For example, if someone says, "It is raining outside," then the statement is true if it is really raining outside. This reality can be ascertained by comparing it with the descriptions below.

Another type is when a statement is consistent with things that are considered valid or are compatible with other observations. First, let's say you hear a marble fall off a table onto the floor. A second person in the room also hears it, and finally, the marble that was on the table is no longer there and is on the floor. These three observations allow us to surmise the marble did indeed fall on the floor, even though it was not seen to do so.

Additionally, an idea or situation can be true if it's useful and motivational to a person. For example, a person might believe that having a good job is the most essential thing in life. The belief is valid for this person and is very useful because the person's actions will be motivated by it. Another person may believe that having a good job isn't the most important thing. This person believes that having good friends is the most essential thing in life. This belief is useful for that person, so it's a true belief for them. Be aware of supposed truths in your life that aren't useful and don't motivate you, for they may not be true at all.

An empirical truth is a truth verified through sensory perception. It is the truth of science and found through rigorous experimentation, measurement observation, and skeptical observation. It follows the scientific method but is used outside of science as well.

Realize that because something happens before an event, doesn't mean it's always the cause of the event. You must root out the problem and search deeply for the truth to make a logical connection between events. Cause and effect requires discernment. Also a problem that endlessly persists should be suspected as a question asked in the wrong way.

You must also be aware of a convenient truth, which is the type of truth people seek when they want to be right when they suspect they may be wrong. It's a truth stated when people assert something is valid when they're not sure or can't be sure it's true. It's gotten from limited research or made up "facts" that support their arguments. This is often the "truth" of insidious propaganda.

Many people go between empirical and convenient truth throughout their day.

Odd Fellowship cannot give you *the* truth. Ultimate truth, like thought, cannot be experienced using the five senses of the actual concrete world. You can't draw a picture of truth or smell or taste it. Truth is an idea, and like all ideas, it isn't of this material realm. Odd Fellowship can, however, teach you some of the great lessons of life. Odd Fellowship can sow seeds in your consciousness through its rituals and charges so that truth can grow. By its influence, radiant truth will light your steps through the paths of error to a bright and unclouded day.

Truth is that magnificent virtue which deals plainly and honestly in all action, without disguise, falsehood, or hypocrisy. It understands all that's wise and good and is the vital spirit of every community founded among human beings.

Truth mingles its unclouded perceptions of duty with the big-hearted grasp of friendship and the sympathizing voice of love. Without truth, society is like a world without a sun. There are towering mountains, the broom-clad vale, the gushing fountain, the broad expanse of ocean lifting its foam-crested billows to the embraces of the skies, and laving with its waters the golden sands of a hundred isles: but overall rests the deformity of darkness if there is no truth.

Without truth the mountain has no greenness; the lovely flower and the enameled vale wear the hue of destruction; the waters sparkle not, and the golden sands on their island-gems send forth no lines of reflected light! TRUTH rises like daylight on the scene, every object floods with beauty and loveliness, and a blessed influence breathes through every portion of society.

The sun is the emblem of power and vigor; the moon and stars aren't only subordinate to it but depend on it. Truth is the great light of Odd Fellowship, just as the sun is the great light of the earth. If you, in the course of your pilgrimage here on earth, realize light's power within your heart, permit it to control your actions, and then reflect its strength on other's hearts. You must, as an Odd Fellow, wed yourself to truth.

Odd-Fellowship teaches its members to be people of truth and honor. Honesty in its broader sense-- of discharging all your duties, both public and private, with scrupulous integrity. Honesty drives from you all dark, crooked, sordid, debasing considerations of self, and substitutes in their place a bolder, loftier, and nobler self. One that will influence you to consider yourself as born not so much for yourself, but also your fellow creatures. There's a higher morality entirely consistent with attention to your affairs--which you shouldn't neglect-- that is the best preparation for an approach in every situation you encounter. It's to this high and noble tone of character that you should aspire.

Some people are ruined because they don't aim at honesty, *but only at the reputation which honesty brings.* Odd Fellowship teaches you to be brave, honest, and diligent. If you have these attributes, victory will crown your efforts.

25. WISDOM

You should follow wisdom and love mercy and truth so you can find favor and good standing in the sight of the universe and society. Wisdom teaches that you should know where evil lurks and stay away from it; that pride, arrogance, evil ways, and a petulant mouth are to be avoided. If you keep the ways of wisdom, you'll be blessed. If you hear wisdom's instruction and are wise--if you watch and wait for its approach--you will find it and live and obtain favor. But if you pay wisdom no mind, refuse to seek it, you'll wrong yourself, and by hating wisdom and knowledge, you'll experience no end of suffering.

With the pursuit of learning comes wisdom. You must study and experience new philosophies and attitudes because your life is short, and the pursuit of knowledge and education can make your life more rewarding. Study your profession in-depth. Learn other languages, experience vibrant cultures, music, or unfamiliar foods. Become conversant in the knowledge you acquire--but don't dominate a conversation with it. Pursue learning and wisdom for your sake--because they add expression and intensity to life.

The mind of a human can be compared to the universe in which it lives. The more you consider the mind's abilities and skill, the more you'll realize the mind is a labyrinth of wonder and amazement. The human mind bears the imprint of sacredness, and pitiful is the person who has traced the human mind through history and not been struck with its power. If mental powers like these now exist, how much more incredible is the force that formed the human mind and put it into operation: each mind on earth all created by and in one great universe.

None will question the fact that every human will have to explain the personal talents the universe assigned to their care and how they improve them and use them to benefit society. You were given talents to make the world a better place, and the universe expects you to use them. It's expected that every Odd Fellow should act under the influence of the solemn charges delivered to them at their initiation, which encourages self-cultivation and improvement of self and community.

Happy is that person who daily reflects on their position in the world and how they will most improve their minds to find comfort in their daily lives and solace in their dying hour. Ask the monk, or philosopher, and they'll both agree that their mentally coherent and happiest moments on earth are when out of control emotions are most subdued, and the mind is calmly left to work out its problems.

The fully developed human mind has been the greatest preserver of society. Some ages seemed to make a greater demand for this element than others. This age of ours is one that yields to none of its forerunners in its call for high intellect. The times' dangers are at hand, and the demand for a high grade of intelligence and great strength of moral principle never was more strong.

New developments of human genius and activity are continually arising, and new dangers to society's dearest interests call for vigilance. This isn't an idle, tame or quiet age. It's an age of activity, enterprise, risks, adventure, philosophizing, and real and pseudo reforms. The age demands intense and mature wisdom. Therefore, study, think, investigate, learn. Collect facts from all sides, pro and con, and then hope to make your decision.

However, remember that it's not knowledge stored up as mental fat which is of value, but the type used as mental muscle. From out of dull and selfish isolation, you must go forward. Regulate with care your fundamental talents and skills. Prove your mental strength, and display it confidently. Deliver yourself from narrowmindedness, your charity from cheapness, your ambitions from smallness. Do and dare, love, and suffer. In this way, you can build a character that will survive the tests which future years or ages bring.

Bear in mind that you're endlessly improvable. It's for the universe to do mighty things quickly, but the universe leaves to humanity the course of growing to greatness slowly bit by bit. To the mind's consciousness, there belong possibilities that are so crucial that no one can study them without being either impressed or made to experience unusual emotions. The conclusion is that every person can become better. By the processes of culture and society to which you can subject yourself, a human being can continuously increase wisdom, strength, and dignity.

You ought to educate yourself forever. You can repeatedly add to the mind's expansion and resources. In all time to come, you can cause it to continue to expand its diameter and latitude. Who can comprehend how great your mental being can become? Who can understand how elevated a life you can live? Who can overrate the vastness of your destiny?

Your mind's abilities are like different rooms within itself, each with a dimension that can't be compared to any physical image ever discovered. The mind's rooms are limitless. As long as you keep these rooms in the process of growth, they will be ready for fresh ideas, beliefs, and opinions. These apartments of the human mind are too awesome to be portrayed by a writer's pen or a painter's brush. Their most distinguishing characteristics are only indicated.

How much knowledge can be found in the rooms of the mind or how many kinds of feelings can they contain? Who can recognize the importance of the traits that have the freedom to grow and bear fruit in them? Who can estimate and experience the joys in them?

To give full expression to the intelligence and capability that resides in the human mind would be equal to picturing the impossible or describing the infinite. Doing either one or the other is useless. Sadly, some people are uninterested in the value of the mind's superior talents, they poorly use them, and attach to their talents weakness. Still, there is never a time when it can't transcend the limits of development to which it has attained. The mind's possessor can educate it forever. All people can learn.

Pretend you're a traveler walking on a road who thinks that the top of the next hill is the end of your journey. No sooner do you arrive at it than you see new ground and other hills beyond it and continue to travel on as before. The mind's improvability is well adapted to revive drooping ambitions. It tends to scatter the gloom resulting from defeated efforts. Let it have a star-like clearness in the consciousness, and there will spring from it an ever-new interest in life and being.

26. CREATIVITY

In another section, you learned that the universe allows an Odd Fellow to create as it creates. Remembering this will create within you the touchstone of genius. You can create experimental work, successful work, and much-failed work, but you must keep going. Be ever mindful not to repeat the same failure again and again. Yet, the only way to go farther in the lodge's work and your life's' work is to go creatively farther in it. The more creative you are in your life and the lodge, the farther you go, which helps protect you from life's fluctuations.

Work hard at being creative.

Exposing yourself to art boosts creativity. When you insert art into your life, your brain begins to reflect on it. Art will teach you to look for meaning, messages, metaphors, and other important information as you proceed through your day. Another reason to integrate art into your life is that it inspires you to work on and improve your own skill, whether that art is how well you do your job, conduct your personal and family life, relate to your friends, or the actual creation of art, music, and drama. This is one reason our emblems and ritual are so important: they bring the creative arts into your consciousness.

Asking questions is another way to improve your productivity, creativity, and personal vision. Asking yourself and others questions about people, places, events, and things give you a curious mind, the glow of enthusiasm, and develops personal curiosity. A healthy attitude toward inquiry empowers you to learn more, make connections that others may not recognize, gather information, and form sound opinions.

In a previous section on learning to know yourself, you discovered that you should pay attention to your daily routine. You might notice that you find yourself following the same routine, but you must question: is this the routine that's the best for you? You must pay attention and notice during the day when and where you're the most productive and work with this knowledge. By embracing the schedule your body wants to follow, you can increase your productivity.

It would help if you also found a way to express the creative ideas that you develop. Doing this will concentrate and intensify your talent and ingenuity. This could be through writing about them or discussing them with a lodge member who will offer only constructive advice. You may also try drawing them out or making a list or chart. But you must find a way to interact with the idea itself as this will give you access to it in the future so other ideas will come more naturally.

Consider going on adventures. As often as possible, move out of what's comfortable to challenge your mind with new perspectives. If travel is possible, do all of it you can. If travel isn't possible, then an adventure may be meeting new people, forcing yourself to encounter new ideas and beliefs about math, science, history, music, philosophy, or literature. Being adventurous gives your mind new possibilities and creates an openness that makes your life and those around you more vibrant and exciting.

Use your five senses to observe your surroundings. Is there music? If there is, how does it affect those listening to it? Pay attention and taste your food so you can identify any complex flavors. What smells do you experience when attending a social event? How does rain feel on your skin?

Exposing yourself to risk is an indispensable feature of improving your creative mind. However, remember that your idea of risk is different from someone else's. In this sense, the risk is again encouraging yourself to step forward out of your typical thinking. Risk gives you the courage to explore your ideas so you can express yourself more thoroughly. Taking a risk means you will fail at some point. But, when you fail, allow no pangs of regret. Steel yourself to failure, learn from it, and move forward to risk again.

27. POVERTY

The road you are journeying can be a rough one. Difficulties might crowd around you to impede your progress. Poverty could fill your path with obstacles that would intimidate a weak spirit. At times, it's a cheerless and dreary way. You may have to deal with poverty and want. But do what you can to keep up your spirits.

When you have enough, remember the hungry and think about poverty and those in need. Study poverty and why it happens, the horrors of it, how it is relieved, and how it affects those who are impoverished. If you should become blessed with abundance, be thankful, not only in words but in deeds. If you have plenty to spare and would be happy to do so, give some of your prosperity in the cause of charity.

In this strangely selfish and uncertain world, none are so rich that they can't end up dependent on others. Money can't purchase some essentials among the commodities of the market. To relieve the pinchings of poverty with clothing, food, and shelter, and send the sunshine of gladness to the poor and needy is something—indeed is much.

Lack of charity isn't the only issue that causes poverty, extreme need, and economic deprivation. The following are some reasons for poverty.

Primarily, poverty is the consequence of the way society is organized. A poorly organized society can't distribute resources properly, whether these resources are financial or other resources such as access to family dwellings, health and community relief, education, and other economic, public, and cultural assistance.

Inequality and intolerance are causes of poverty. Gender inequality, caste systems, or prejudice based on race, religion, sexual orientation, or tribal affiliation creates situations with no avenue to resources needed for a society to design full and productive lives for its citizens.

Not every government in the world can or will assist people who need healthcare or food. Without a social safety net, there's nothing to prevent families from sliding even further into poverty. In these areas, benevolent organizations like the Independent Order of Odd Fellows must meet their needs.

Large prolonged outbreaks of disease, warfare, violence, and natural disasters are causes of poverty. These afflictions destroy social infrastructure, force society to grind to a halt, and cause people to flee their homes instead of feeding themselves or holding jobs.

You probably know that poverty causes hunger, yet you might not know that hunger is also a cause of poverty. A lack of food causes malnutrition, which affects the immune system. People become sicker, and it becomes harder for them to work. Less work means less money and more poverty. Extreme poverty and poor health go hand in hand, and if sound healthcare systems don't exist, that too causes more poverty because of the sickness caused by lack of food.

Countless people who don't have a decent education also live in economic deprivation. This is why an Odd Fellow must internalize the notion that the mind is continuously improvable. There are many situations where education is denied or discouraged for those on the receiving end of prejudice. In many countries, women aren't allowed an education, which dooms them from the start to a life of poverty. In many countries, systems of prejudice make it harder for certain groups to improve themselves.

Inadequate public works and infrastructure make it difficult for people to travel to and from work. Not having access to communications or electricity or decent roads and bridges can isolate communities and the transportation of goods and services, resulting in acute hardship.

International sanctions on a country create an extreme need among the sanctioned country's inhabitants. When sanctions are put in place, other foreign governments can't invest in the sanctioned country or import goods for sales such as medical supplies and food. Then the people in those countries suffer from hunger and economic problems.

Those who have a physical or mental disability are more likely to experience poverty. Performing routine tasks is difficult for some disabled; thus, working certain jobs becomes more difficult. This could make it difficult for many disabled people to find good-paying jobs to generate enough income to stay out of poverty.

Having no family support also creates poverty. Being part of a family creates a safety net in case of difficult times. Families can also serve as networks for job hunting and are available for good advice. If someone is not in contact with their family, they can become more susceptible to poverty.

Many of the world's poorest nations were former colonies from which resources were systematically extracted to benefit colonizing countries. For most of these former colonies, colonialism and its legacies have helped create the conditions that prevent many people from accessing land, capital, education, and other resources that allow people to support themselves adequately. In these nations, poverty is one legacy of a troubled history involving conquest.

Another cause of poverty is rampant government corruption. The people in power in a country divert funds for their personal acquisitions instead of spending the money on education, infrastructure, or healthcare for society.

The lie of worthlessness creates poverty. Poor people often believe they are failures. And this message of oppression and hopelessness affects their ability to hope for a better future. Their grandfathers lived in poverty. Their fathers lived in poverty. The cycle continues with them and they believe it will continue to the next generation as well. When people believe this lie of poverty and believe they are worthless because of their circumstances, they become victims. They lose hope, and without hope, it's difficult to dream of a better way and almost impossible to be an agent for positive change.

When people in poverty have a low view of themselves and no hope for the future, their personal and social relationships are affected. They have a low regard for other people and don't believe that their personal and social relationships will get better. Children are particularly vulnerable to this lie. When poverty surrounds them, they assume they have no value or purpose. Those in this situation need valuable examples of success and templates on how to achieve it. They do not need rehearsed answers and patronizing solutions. They need guidance and step by step instruction, *developed within their cultural standards*, on overcoming the horrors they face. They need information on interpersonal relationships and how society works in order to be successful.

Be aware these solutions must fit into another's cultural perspectives. It is not effective to provide solutions by using your culture to override another.

Why is it necessary to know what causes poverty? Because it helps the Odd Fellow locate where help is needed the most so the Order can supply relief to those in distress.

28. DEALING WITH PEOPLE

Care for your enemies, understand why they are the way they are so that you may pity them, and so you may not become as they are. If someone curses you, do them a good turn if it is expedient, but hold your peace regarding them if possible unless their behavior is unlawful. Because often, when someone curses you publicly, they usually damage themselves more than you. When your enemy is making a fool of themselves, don't interrupt them.

Be aware that as you move toward your goals in life, the more your enemies will come forward to prevent you from reaching them. Your enemies may be other people. But your enemies can also be yourself: too much mirth, revelry, pride, ambition, or the hunt for worldly fame and glory. These things will bring temporary pleasure, and because the fun is short-lived, you'll seek them again and again. Here is the danger: you will pursue them continuously for the pleasurable addictive effect, which could throw off your delicate life balance.

Don't repeat things that are told to you, and you shall never fare worse. Whether it be friend or foe, don't talk of other people's lives. If you have heard words about another, be bold and let them die with you, you won't burst by keeping them to yourself. Be fair, especially to people who confide in you. Keep their secrets more carefully, even than your own. Watch over their interests, and promote their welfare with the vigilance of a sentinel in the presence of armed enemies.

Good conduct only, not mere affirmations and appearances, can bring the approval and confidence of the ethical and wise. But let the Odd Fellow add to goodness and prudence. Let caution watch your lips and your ways. We would say to him: "Bestow not your confidence too hastily. Be just to yourself as well as generous to others."

You need personal boundaries in your life. Personal boundaries are limits you set with other people. Odd Fellows sometimes need to set personal limits because of the nature of the relief work we do. Community work and helping the underprivileged can be mentally exhausting.

You must know your limits. Be attentive to which things other people do that bother you or create stress in your life. You should take good care of yourself. Don't be shy about admitting this. The Good Samaritan was able to help because he practiced his own mental, physical, and financial self-care that made him able to save a life.

To set boundaries, you need to clearly define your intellectual, emotional, and physical limits with strangers, friends, family, colleagues, and intimate partners. Be as precise as possible about what these boundaries are. Next, decide on consequences if your boundaries are violated and be consistent in enforcing them. Be accurate and thorough with your explanations and gentle in your admonishment.

Admonish a friend if needed. It could be that your friend has done nothing, but if they have, they won't do it again. It may be they didn't say it. But if they did, they won't repeat it. There are people who slip in their speech but haven't slipped in their hearts. And who hasn't accidentally offended someone? Admonish your neighbor or friend first. Give you both a chance to discuss before becoming angry. Don't lay up anger, because it builds and multiplies and spills over as a hot liquid--all over everything. Express your concerns as you go along with gentle admonishment.

When discussing a problematic issue with a person, don't attack their character but instead denounce their argument. Don't misrepresent or exaggerate a person's statement to make it easier to criticize and don't allow them to do it to you.

Avoid outshining your employer or any person in authority over you. This was a lesson that David learned in dealing with Saul. Many people dislike the successes of others and some in positions of authority detest a subordinate outshining them. A person in authority rarely defers to a subordinate that's viewed as being more intelligent than them. A powerful person believes they are sovereign and while they may not mind being helped they may not tolerate being surpassed. Advise them in a way that jogs their memory rather than outperforming them or making them look ignorant.

Hold on to clever assistants and friends. This was a lesson Saul should have learned in dealing with David. A person in a position of leadership must learn to lean on persons of understanding who can protect them from every ignorance and difficulty.

Justice, temperance, and charity are the duties of all Odd Fellows. You should be just in your dealings with the Order and with the world. You should be diligent and honest. You should be kind in your demeanor to all with whom you come in contact. You should feel compassion for those in sorrow; you should bind up the broken heart, comfort the downhearted, and dry the tears of the bereaved.

You must weigh your conduct and your actions and allow the balance to be a just one. The spirit of justice won't permit you to impose false balances. If you have erred, you must not shield yourself, but instead, admit your wrongdoing and fix it if you can, then don't repeat the event. Don't protect other people who do wrong, however much they play on your sympathy--be wise to manipulation. If a person is a habitual troublemaker, allow the universe to compensate them for their evil. Better one suffers than many.

The manipulator seeks to avoid confronting their wrongs, avoid responsibility, and avoid changing their ways. As we have already seen, change is a law of the universe, yet the manipulator seeks, unsuccessfully, to avoid change, which multiplies their suffering. They also strive to put you on the defensive or to make you doubt yourself and your perceptions.

Manipulators will maliciously lie to confuse you or lie to get you to do what they want. A manipulator will deny knowing about previous agreements and promises. They will also deny their past behavior. A manipulator will avoid being confronted or taking responsibility at all costs, or shift the blame for their wrong to another person. They will also play the victim to elicit sorrow and guilt from others.

When dealing with a manipulator and you feel the situation is unsafe, remove yourself from the circumstance. If you deal with them, initiate a conversation without being contentious. Arguing over facts is usually unproductive, but you should do your best to express what you believe. Personal boundaries are essential with manipulators.

29. ADDICTIONS

Being addicted to substances, certain vices, or unhealthy relationships (yes, one can become addicted to a person) indicates that you need assistance. You should work to be level headed and keep your mental balance. During these trials, you must remain focused so that you can admit you need assistance or advice to deal with these addictions. If it's practical, seek advice and counsel from a member of the Order--ask them for help and support--they can't turn you away. Ask them to stand with you. Ask them to be there when they can. Listen to their counsel. Not asking for help when you're an addict will result in many grievous evils, and you may come to poverty and rags, both in the mental realm and in the physical one.

Addictions come in many forms. Addiction to substances, to work, to food, and unhealthy people or relationships for example. Some people call bad relationships "love," when in reality they are an addiction. Accepting change and using your own ability to create change is key to helping with addiction. You should be prepared to change who you socialize with, avoid things associated with the addiction, change how you deal with stress, and positively change how you think about yourself. You must also be prepared to seek professional guidance if needed.

Your lodge members will help all they can, but you need to give to the lodge in return. An Odd Fellow must never take advantage of their lodge.

30. ODD FELLOWS STAND AGAINST BIGOTRY

IOOF NON-DISCRIMINATION POLICY

The Independent Order of Odd Fellows (I.O.O.F.) will not discriminate against any individual on the basis of disability, age other than that of minimum to join the Order (lodge, club or group), ethnicity, gender, race, sexual orientation, religion, or other social identity. The I.O.O.F. will make reasonable modifications in policies, practices, or procedures when such modifications are necessary to afford its services and facilities to individuals with disabilities, unless the modifications would fundamentally alter the nature of its services. The I.O.O.F. will not exclude any individual based on disability, age, ethnicity, gender, race, sexual orientation, religion, or other social identity from the full and equal enjoyment of its services and facilities, unless the individual poses a direct threat to the health or safety of others, or him/herself, that cannot be eliminated by a modification of policies, practices, or procedures or by the provision of auxiliary aids or services. The I.O.O.F. will not exclude any individual from the full and equal enjoyment of its services and facilities because of the individual's association with a person of disability, age, ethnicity, gender, race, sexual orientation, religion or other social identity.

--Independent Order of Odd Fellows Code of Laws

Odd Fellowship observes tolerance, because the word tolerance is discussed in our ritual. Found throughout the ritual is the notion of a universal family. Worldwide cooperation between all people isn't possible with bigotry in your heart. Don't let prejudice control you when dealing with people. Don't blemish your good work by using uncomfortable words when you help others. Educate yourself before you speak; before you judge another, examine yourself, and on the day of trouble, you'll find mercy.

If you're intolerant toward others who are unlike you, either renounce your bigotry or renounce Odd Fellowship--for no person can serve both of these causes. It is possible to dislike one person because of their personality or behavior. But don't accuse their entire social or cultural group, or those with the same disability, gender, race, religion, or sexual orientation of the same characteristics or behavior as the person you dislike. Doing so is a lie you have made up to hide from a deep self-hatred found in yourself. In this case, the problem is yourself, not others. A discriminatory attitude shows a stultified mind and a stooped intellect.

Accusing a particular group of bigotry to allow yourself discriminatory thoughts and actions is unacceptable and provides no cover for discrimination. Some may ask, "Shouldn't the Order tolerate my dislike or hatred for a certain cultural group or religion? By not tolerating my hatred, aren't the Odd Fellows being intolerant?"

No.

We can't extend acceptance to those full of hatred toward a religion, skin color, or specific cultures. We must defend society against the aggression of intolerant people who encourage racial or cultural violence, eugenics, torture, slavery, ethnic cleansing, or brutal persecution of certain groups. Not standing against this guarantees the end of tolerance. Those who are tolerant will disappear, and the idea of tolerance with them. The social compact, as mentioned in ritual, is only possible when there is tolerance practiced. The Order is built around tolerance as demonstrated in our degrees and is implied throughout the ritual.

Human prejudice, bigotry, and intolerance have been the cause of more misery in the world than all other evils combined. Their power must be destroyed by asserting and maintaining the birthright of human equality. You must regard and treat all as your equal. The universe has created us all in like form. We're all made of the same dust, and it rains on both the honest and dishonest--for the universe sees us equally as created beings.

Confronting prejudice is essential, for you never know when another might turn and use prejudice against you. For, one day you may find an advantage because of who you are or what you represent, and the next, your advantage may vanish as snow when the thaw comes, and you can find yourself against the spear tip of prejudice. Confronting prejudice protects us all.

It would be best if you confronted prejudice wherever you find it, whether it's in yourself or others. When you confront prejudicial statements and actions, you'll find fewer prejudicial words and activities. Confronting prejudice also makes you feel more competent and less regretful. Saying nothing in response to prejudice creates an uncomfortable feeling of hypocrisy, and you may be judged harshly by those who endure bigotry or seek to stamp it out. Remember, we're an Order of tolerance striving for universal sisterhood and brotherhood.

An Odd Fellows lodge or an Odd Fellow that is found to be bigoted will become known. Be sure you will be found out.

31. BEING TACTFUL

One of the essences of Odd Fellowship is realizing
that it involves encounter and engagement with something or
someone of whom you are profoundly ignorant. This is why
tact is so important.

Tact is something in a person that enables them to
know the character of the person they meet and how to deal
with them delicately. It is being considerate of others. A tactful
Odd Fellow feels a person's personality automatically and
knows what makes them happy. Everyone has this ability to
some extent, but in some, it's almost like divine inspiration.

Being tactful in the lodge is an essential part of
membership.

Now and then, you'll meet some persons entirely void
of tact. They enjoy being someone who "tells it like it is," or as
someone who is "brutally honest." They say what's on their

mind with "no filter." Their actions are grotesque, foolish, and generally make others uncomfortable. Their words may not be related to the person or situation and are often unimportant and irritating. The tactless person may learn about the rules but not about the hearts of others. They may know human nature in general but not be able to recognize one person from another. A disrespectful person often makes others do or say the wrong things.

The person of tact sees the differences between people. They read the character of people in their looks, expressions, words, and general bearing. A tactful person doesn't see anything shocking or disagreeable in others, whether a disability, race, religion or sexual orientation. They don't remind others of unpleasant issues. The tactful person does you a favor in a way to make you think you are doing them a favor by allowing them to do it.

To be tactful, consider your words carefully and think before you speak. In a conversation consider another person's viewpoint and actively listen to what they're saying--respond to them. Consider any cultural differences between you: age, race, religion, where they were raised, where they come from etc., and be careful to not say anything disrespectful. Be gracious when you're irritated and politely remove yourself from any situation that is negative.

As far as anger is concerned it's something a tactful person keeps under control. Whenever possible let cold deliberation take the place of an angry outburst. The first step is to realize you're angry which sets the stage for reigning it in. Determine why you feel you need the anger and determine how mad you are on a scale of one to ten. Then let it wane.

Begin to pay attention to the situation you are in and focus intently on everything you say and everything you do. Know how and when to stop your anger. It is a sign of strength to keep your head when other fools have lost theirs.

If you cultivate tact, you will enjoy knowing people's quality and how to deal with them happily and helpfully. This is important for an Odd Fellow who is working with a community project. You must study people diligently, and it requires empathy, but developing tact is well worth the effort.

32. WHAT IS WITHIN YOUR CONTROL AND ACCEPTANCE

In your life when dealing with any emotionally strenuous issues, you should identify what's within your power to control and what isn't. Spend time examining the differences between the two. Using the concept of *truth,* honestly identify what you can and cannot control in your life. Understand its applicability to any issue you encounter. What's within your ability to control? Can you really control what another person does or control their personality? What's not in your control will create emotional and perhaps physical pain if you even try. It would be best if you stopped struggling to affect that which isn't in your power to control.

Comprehending these two principles of attitude will only be useful if you internalize them and come to believe them. It is only at this point, you'll be able to put them into action, and even then, you can only strengthen them with practice. One way to do this is to examine the Opening of the Lodge ritual. Each officer from Inside Guardian to Noble Grand has their duties and powers explained in detail, and at no time are they to exceed them. It is not within their ability to do so. Every new situation that arises will require you to ask yourself if you're viewing the problem clearly and *truthfully*. Examine whether there are personal false or selfish thoughts that are interfering with reality as it *truly* is.

For example, can a rock found on a roadway be good or bad? To describe a rock, one might state, "this rock throws well, so it's good for that." But extending the notion of "a good throwing rock" to make a judgment about the rock as a whole is to go too far. While it is *accurate* and fair to say "this rock is good for throwing," to say "this is a good rock" is to allege that your personal judgments matter more than the *truth*.

For a rock-- independent of human judgment--can't be "good" or "bad." It has no personality because it isn't alive. Your thoughts and conclusions are interfering with the rock as it truly is. A rock is just a rock. Perceiving the rock in this way, you are developing the skill of sound judgment, and it puts into practice the fundamental principles mentioned in the preceding paragraphs.

At this point, prepare yourself to practice the skill of acceptance. Accept whatever you're faced with, whether it is good or bad. To accept is to acknowledge whatever is happening in your life. You don't say "yes" or "no" to it but instead, say "I understand." You can't stop a devastating flood from happening. You can't keep a storm from destroying your town. Saying to yourself "I understand" helps keep you focused here and now.

33. SOCIAL DIVISIONS

The evils that hurt society and people should be, in a way, considered your own. If you physically or mentally injure another, you will hurt yourself: either your reputation, your physical body, or your mind. Whatever directly affects a part of the body must involve the entire structure. In the same way, society's misfortunes are your misfortunes, and its sufferings are yours. If famine is in the land you'll starve. If disease is rampant you will be ill.

Humanity and societies are divided into numerous sects and parties holding distinctive opinions. However absurd or ridiculous each may seem to the other, its devotees are mostly sincere and firm in their belief. The Christian's faith isn't more earnest and optimistic than the Jew's, Muslim's, Wiccan's, Hindu's, or Buhddist's. All of these groups hold the opinion that they are correct and can produce arguments in support of their theories, which, in their view, are clear and conclusive.

Each of these groups is divided into scores of even *more* sects and parties that may be so opposed to each other they are in constant controversy. To the disgrace of the spirit of love, they often conduct their disputes with bitterness that would much better suit "sinners" than followers of the peaceful deities they profess to follow.

This same lesson may be applied to anything with which humanity interacts: politics, athletics, music, film, architecture, literature, art, and so on. All these have numerous sects and parties within them, holding different beliefs about every single topic. This is why one should never believe that all people of one group share the same opinion. This is the danger of bigotry, as mentioned in another section.

As no two people among billions of humans look alike, so perhaps no two in this vast multitude of minds think alike. A difference of opinion, especially on religious or political subjects, has always existed and will continue to divide our hearts until we reach universal peace and respect among all parties, sects, and nations. Should you despise another for these differences? No. They have the same right as you to the enjoyment of their opinion, and they have the right to keep it in opposition to the views of the whole world as long as no one is hurt.

34. FOCUS, CONCENTRATION, AND LEARNING

"Strait is the gate and narrow the way that leads to life." This adage, or another similarly written, is found in many other traditions and mystical teachings. One of the meanings of the maxim is to teach "focus."

The word "Strait" in the quote is used in the archaic sense and means "narrow." Interpret the part which says "that leads to life," as meaning "that leads to success." Or, if you prefer, "that leads to a better existence."

So what are we left with? We're left with a statement which teaches that focusing on a goal is essential to being successful. The focus must be narrow and precise without wandering away from your objective. Most people don't understand how vital focus is when you're attempting to achieve a goal. Your focus must be "strait" at the gate, and your path "narrow" as you move forward toward your goal.

One of the first keys to learning focus is to learn to concentrate for extended lengths of time. An excellent way to practice this is memorizing lodge floor work. This is why, when you join a lodge, it's essential to move through the chairs and learn the parts for each chair. The time spent memorizing parts and lodge floor work is designed to increase your concentration. As you memorize your parts, pay attention to and examine how you learn and, in turn, the way you think. By reviewing your learning and thought process, you'll gain an insight into knowing yourself.

If you enjoy listening as a way to learn, you prefer to learn by being told what to do. You may enjoy lectures and speeches, storytelling, recordings, videos, and having someone tell you what to do next in the learning process. A reader would be a person who prefers to learn from notes, books, or other reading material at their own pace.

If you are a writer, you learn by making notes about what you're learning. Do these notes in your own words. Writing allows you to rephrase and think about what you're learning. If you enjoy talking with others, then you'll probably prefer to learn through discussion. A part of learning through dialogue is listening and then challenging or questioning what you hear until you understand it.

You may be a person who prefers to learn by watching. You like to be shown how to do something, to see examples of what works and what doesn't, then imitate what you've seen. Finally, you may prefer to learn by doing. If you learn this way, you learn through trying something out and deciding what does and doesn't work for you.

You probably have a dominant way of learning and then a few other less prevalent ways. It's important when learning something new to approach learning in various ways so that you can fully grasp your material. You may need to use all examples above to learn something. Or, you may find that you learn about technology best by listening, gardening by writing, or job related things by reading. Just pay attention to yourself and analyze the approaches that fit best for you.

35. NATURE AND ITS IMPORTANCE IN ODD FELLOWSHIP

Nature has been the Odd Fellow's teacher from the beginning. Ritual makes clear that nature is full of emblems that lead to truth. Nature has furnished us material to serve as a foundation to all the sciences, from astronomy to botany, geology, and chemistry. Nature has trained us in our search for truth. Learning the laws of measurement, force, and life forms leads to truth and disciplining the mind for inquiry. Nature also trains the mind to reason.

Suppose you take a survey of the beautiful works of creation, and closely examine everything around you and consider their nature and characteristics. In that case, your most intense respect will be inspired by learning about the superb order and proportions that nature entails. The science of astronomy lifts your mind above the world and its doings. The sun, the center of our solar system, brings light and heat to the world. The starry skies are composed of thousands of suns that are centers of other systems. Comets fly through space for what purpose we know not. The seasons are regular and unchanged. The tide ebbs and flows. The earth gives out its abundance to supply humanity's wants.

Nature furnishes raw material for the arts. Stones and trees inspire our architectural ideas; marble allows the sculptor to create the human form's beauty. Nature's colors and scenes inspire the painter's genius and give them the instrument to achieve their ideas. Nature's sound touches the music in humanity's soul and enables us to sing it out in music's varied speech. Natural scenes are the chief pleasure of the poet and enter into their verse.

The laws of nature demonstrate that "sameness" underlies "otherness." That which grabs the attention is the "otherness" or diversity, which leads us to believe that otherness also means "separateness." But an examination of natural laws shows very clearly the same rules apply to all things, whether they appear to be different or not. If we search the sky, we will see endless diversity in the shapes of clouds. Even though the universe allows for individuality, the same natural laws apply to each cloud.

Nature trains the philosopher that looks behind creation as they ask how and why this all came about. Nature encourages those who work the soil to study its structure, and those who dig out treasure from veins within the earth must acquaint themselves with the various mineral substances. The natural environment is an instructor to the mind and forces the mind to be orderly in its action, and it trains the eye to have an accurate observation.

Nature can't see its own patterns. Plants can hardly move, let alone think. Yet, in essence, each plant contains within itself a microcosm of the whole of nature. As humans, we possess many of the same patterns found in nature within our minds and bodies. Because they are inside of us, we look for them in the natural world and are delighted by their presence. These patterns are so apparent and so attractive because they run deep, almost as deep as the roots of the tree of life itself. Patterns are universal, and because they are in us: mind and body, we look and see them in nature as well.

An examination of your hand will tell the story. Examine your hand, and you will find the wrinkles on your knuckles composed of minute squares and triangles that resemble cracked mud on a dry riverbank, the cells of a plant under a microscope, the street grid of an unplanned city, or the veiny parts of a leaf. The brain also has similar designs.

Sunflowers have spirals where the seeds are packed tightly in a Fibonacci sequence. We also see the spiral in the way limbs grow in a spiral pattern up the trunk of a tree or in the coil of a serpent. You will find this shape on your fingertips in the swirls of your fingerprints. Rivers and highways remind us of the veins and arteries in our bodies. What's inside of us is also outside of us.

The effect of nature on our character is varied. In nature, we find the love and care of the universe and what it puts into creation. Scientists find their instruction in nature, and the artist finds material for work and sustenance for their sense of beauty. The universe, as it creates, not only makes the beautiful but adapts it to our tastes. At first, we define taste as one of our five senses, and it teaches us desire, discernment, delight or disgust--something all five senses are designed to do. Nature awakens a passion for the beautiful unless we approach it as a butcher approaches a lamb for dissection. Nature inspires art of all kinds, that of the poet, the painter, and the musician.

Every personality is unique. Nature arms each person with skills that enable them to do something impossible to others. A great tendency of modern life is to attempt to eradicate individuality. But the great duty you owe yourself is to preserve and develop it. You shouldn't allow your education, place of employment, or your environment to rob you of your distinctive personality.

The trouble with many is that we are content to be echoes or mere copies of other people. But no two humans are alike so that no one can take the place of another, nor can they do quite as easily or quite as well the thing another person can do. It's futile and disastrous to try and mold yourself to a different pattern than what nature intended for you. Whatever you are, or whatever you do, be yourself--be an original--as long as you aren't hurting or violating the rights of another person.

You may often think that if you had another person's means, or ability, or opportunity, you could do something worth doing. But be aware this is the creeping power of envy and its confining chains. Nature encourages you to improve your opportunity with the possessions and abilities it has given to you. It's a good thing for you to do the best you can do just where and as you are.

Familiarity with nature in its various moods is a noble privilege and one easily pursued. One who lives in the country has this privilege to the full. There's something in every country scene to attract and charm the mind. Some beauty awaits the seeing eye, even in the most desolate place. Even in a city, you'll find nature. Parks that please the eye and rest the spirit; lawns that bloom in the beauty of various colors, the nearby country areas that invite afternoon trips, nearby rivers, creeks, and lakes are all ways to connect to the lessons of the third degree. No Odd Fellow needs to be a stranger to nature.

You may not have realized it, but much of what you have read in this book and seen in the ritual revolves around the scientific notion that everything in the universe functions in an orderly symmetrical manner. A substantial amount of information you have received both in the lodge and this book is about the scientific law of cause and effect. If you do good things, good things can happen. If you help society, other good things can happen. "I have never seen the righteous begging bread," "It is better to give than receive," "Do unto others as you would have them do unto you," "Love thy neighbor as thyself." These statements may be found in the teachings of all the major and minor religions, although phrased differently and in different languages. Their cautions are as old as humanity.

In nature, for every cause, there will be an effect. The effects aren't always precisely the same except on paper. In reality, when dealing with community problems, there are so many conditions existing resulting from other causes and effects that interact with each other that conditions are always changing. Cause and effect are the drivers of transformation in nature.

36. THE GOLDEN RULE FOR ODD FELLOWS

Another admirable feature connected with The Independent Order of Odd Fellows is that it cultivates moral feelings. A just sense of another's privileges and rights is an attainment of invaluable worth among humanity. It is a virtue that all commend, yet it is one which too few practice.

The Golden Rule dates from at least the Confucious times (550-479 BCE), and can be phrased a few different ways:

1. Do unto others as you would have them do unto you.

2. Treat others as you would like others to treat you.

3. Do not treat others in a way that you would not want to be treated.

4. What you wish on others, you wish on yourself.

5. Regard your neighbor's gain as your own gain and your neighbor's loss as your loss.

The Golden Rule is the principle of treating others as you want to be treated. It is a maxim found in many belief systems, religions, and cultures. It can be considered an ethic of reciprocity in some belief systems, although some treat it differently.

Many of us wish that everyone else would follow our own personal principles. To some extent, most of us believe that everyone should follow our beliefs and that our personal views should be everyone's views. But since we're all different, coming from diverse cultural, social, and religious backgrounds, there can be no possible agreement that your ideas are the best for each person on earth.

In dealing with other people and societies, you may seek to push your beliefs on others. You may try to persuade them or convert them to your way of believing. Some of those you attempt to convert will be convinced to see things your way if you share several other values. Others will resist you, or try to convert you to *their* way of believing. All these attempts at converting creates a foundation for the use of force, oppression, and power. Through the use of argument, tyranny, violence, or war--people hope that their beliefs and principles will win the day while destroying others.

The Golden Rule is a universal law that doesn't take sides with or contend with competing personal values. It doesn't contain a creed. It bids each to their own rule, aside from the advantages and successes in their personal life.

The Golden Rule is a principle that can appeal to all people. Instead of attacking the values, behavior, and very being of others, we are offered a new aspect. The Golden Rule bids you to expand your vision, see yourself in new relationships. It asks you to transcend the walls you've built against others, see yourself in the place of others, and see others in your place. It asks you to examine your values. If you disapprove of the way another treats you, after you treated them badly to begin with, shouldn't that make you reexamine your values?

Odd Fellowship teaches that all situations of power are temporary and precarious. You may find yourself robust financially and socially at one point in your life, while another is doing poorly because of certain circumstances. As you also know, this situation may reverse at any moment, and you'll find yourself doing poorly while at the same time, the other is powerful in their finances, job, or social situations.

Attacking the values, beliefs, and principles *of another* requires the use of power and oppression in your attack. Defending *your* values, ideas, and principles requires power and oppression in your defense.

The Golden Rule doesn't require the use of power and oppression toward another person or society. It doesn't require the ability to resist or defend against another.

The use of the Golden Rule goes far deeper into the great truth that power so often ignores and, in the end, destroys it: when you mistreat others, you sabotage yourself. You disconnect yourself from others, from the understanding of them, and from self knowledge. You insulate yourself from the goodness in others making it more difficult for them to assist you. You narrow your values resulting in mental imprisonment, and cut yourself off from what you and they have in common. This commonness is more lasting and more gratifying than what you possess by insulating yourself from others. You separate yourself from the Friendship, Love, and Truth that's available from humanity. And for all your power, you weaken yourself. This is why when you have power, *fear is such a close companion.* Fear is always the companion of power.

Insulation from others is the disease that erodes The Golden Rule. We insulate ourselves from others when we think "I'm right; I have the truth. If you differ from me, you're an outcast, and you're ignorant." When this belief becomes the dominant disease between groups, each group will believe they are absolutely correct, and the struggle over power begins.

We can argue that the greatest evils inflicted by humans on other humans aren't done by self-seekers, pleasure lovers, or the amoral, but by hot-blooded supporters of certain ethical principles. They are bound body and soul to some larger purpose: the "nation," the "race," the "masses," the "party," the "religion," etc. In the heat of devotion to the larger purpose, there is the fanaticism that wears away and finally destroys all that links a person to shared humanity.

In the name of their cause, they will torture, starve, and trample underfoot millions upon millions of their fellow humans. In the name of their cause, they will cultivate the foulest treachery. And when their methods fail, as they always do, they are prepared to destroy their cause or their own people rather than accept the reality of defeat.

The Golden Rule doesn't solve ethical problems for an Odd Fellow but instead offers a way to approach them. It doesn't tell us the exact way to treat others; it doesn't give us a list of detailed steps but shows us a theory or the spirit in which we should treat people.

For example, the criminal wants a judge to set him free, but a law requires otherwise. Instead, to follow the Golden Rule, the judge will give full consideration to the conditions under which the criminal acted, try to understand the criminal, and do what a judge can to help the criminal while protecting society from the dangers the lawbreaker poses.

Trying to live according to the Golden Rule means trying to empathize, suffer with, or relate to other people, including those who may be very different from you. Empathy is at the root of kindness, compassion, understanding, and respect – qualities that we all appreciate whoever we are, whatever we think, and from wherever we come. Although it isn't possible to know what it feels like to be a different person or live in other circumstances and have different life experiences, it isn't difficult for you to imagine what would cause you suffering. So, you should avoid causing suffering to others.

This is a virtue that's insisted on by Odd Fellowship. All members are encouraged not to embroil themselves with any who, through ignorance, or even bitterness would defame the order. The doctrine that others have the same right to their opinions as we have to ours is kept continuously in view. Each is required and prompted to square his life by the Golden Rule, "As ye would that others should do unto you, do ye even so unto them." Here the moral feelings are brought directly under the teaching of the best world religions have to offer..

If such instruction is only theory, it might pass like other teachings given to the world; it might garnish many a page and comparatively few lives. But here, it's reduced under a regulating system to practice. It not only exacts toleration and charity, but it sets the Odd Fellow at once to act on the Golden Rule's principles.

The Odd Fellows acknowledge the beauty and fitness of the theory. The Order says to them, go and practice it, and learn the reality of its enjoyment. They accordingly commence at once their work — contributing to the needy, and by the practice acquires the habit of active benevolence.

An early step in being an Odd Fellow is learning the luxury there is in doing good. "That it is more blessed to give than it is to receive." The Odd Fellow now advances another step and talks of the recipients of her bestowments. They find it true in this case, as in every other, "where the treasure is, there will the heart be also." They take an interest in the welfare of those around them, which they never felt before. They begin to look at the human race with other eyes and feel for them with another heart; so that in the discharge of the personal offices enjoined by the Order, they find their mind fitted for the delicate duty devolving on them.

37. LIVING WITH UNCERTAINTY AS AN ODD FELLOW

What if the delicate and intricate mechanism of your mind is out of gear? What if you're battling anxiety, depression, worry, or loneliness? A secret sorrow swells and sways in your heart, and you cry: "Who will show me goodness? Who will help remove my many sorrows? What Good Samaritan can help bring relief to my dazed and confused mind?" It's here that members of the three links bring to bear their tremendous power. If it's true "that one touch of nature makes the whole world kin," it's equally valid that the ties of brother and sisterhood here would wield their most potent influence. Of the faithful Odd Fellow, it may be said, "They have a tear for pity, and a hand open as day for charity."

Uncertainty is the only certainty there is, and learning to live with insecurity *is* security. Uncertainty exists to teach you a lesson: that we human beings aren't in control of our lives. It is a reminder that the universe is in control, and it relieves us of having to make many tough decisions in our lives. Events that need to happen to or for us may be decisions that humanity would find distasteful or heartbreaking to make. So the universe makes them to spare us that part of suffering, perhaps leaving us to suffer less.

If you feel uncertain, it may be a product of your thinking more about your future than about the moment in which you find yourself.

You have no way of knowing if you'll get employment, whether your actions will result in success or failure, or if your relationship will survive or fade. But you can deal with uncertainty a little easier.

First, consider living only one day at a time. Make your plans for the day either the night before or the morning on waking. Then focus only on what you may do today. Give no thought for tomorrow, only for today. You may wish to set 10 minutes aside in your day for a period of worrying--for example, from 8:00 to 8:10 pm. If worries pop up during your day, decide to worry during that time. If you forget to worry during this period, then you must wait until then next time the next day, and so on.

An Odd Fellow should identify and remove unproductive worries. Productive worrying will produce plans and ways of dealing with the situation at hand. Useless worrying will make you feel too anxious and uncertain. You may need to write about your worries and identify those you can plan to overcome and those you cannot. Then remove the unproductive concerns by focusing on the problems you have developed plans to overcome.

Understanding the Guardians' roles in the lodge is an important step in dealing with worries and unwanted thinking. Again, you're encouraged to view the lodge officers' roles and adapt them to controlling and working with your thoughts.

Another way to deal with uncertainty in your life is to create new habits and methods for doing things. These will give you a feeling of control in your life. They also become something new to focus on. Create as much structure as you can in your life during uncertain times. You can see the importance of structure in the way a lodge conducts meetings. Keep in mind that some people prefer more structure than others. You have to decide on the proper amount for yourself while balancing the desire to manage uncertainty.

One of the older emblems of the Order is "the wise owl." Using the wise old owl to help live with uncertainty is a good idea.

To understand the wise owl, we need to talk about the human brain. Two parts of the human brain are the prefrontal cortex and the amygdala.

The prefrontal cortex brain region involves complex thinking behavior, personality expression, decision making, moderating social behavior and focusing one's attention. The prefrontal cortex is our learning, reasoning, and thinking center of the brain—it is the part of the brain that can see the big picture. It helps you control your impulses, focus your attention, and also helps regulate emotions. It can also help predict the consequences of one's actions and anticipate events in the immediate environment.

The amygdala is essential to your ability to feel certain emotions and to perceive them in other people. This includes fear and the many changes that fear causes in the body. When you live with uncertainty, the amygdala can become a hyperactive watchdog. It constantly barks--never letting up-- over threats that may not be there.

We've all dealt at one time with a dog, whether ours or someone else's, that seems to bark and bark for no reason. Your amygdala isn't so good at figuring out if something is truly a threat. Stress, worry, frustration, or anger can cause your amygdala to work overtime. It instinctually causes you to react to situations without using your rational or thinking centers of the brain. The amygdala is your barking watchdog, continually keeping you on the alert, denying you peace, sleep, and relaxation, when there is no danger to you at all.

One key to living with uncertainty is recognizing when your watchdog is barking and warning about things that aren't a threat. You should quiet it and lead yourself with the wisdom of the wise owl. When your body and brain are calm, you are better able to access your prefrontal cortex. Viewing your emotions and experiences through the eye of the prefrontal cortex, you can respond to situations more mindfully instead of reacting to them emotionally.

Living with uncertainty requires confidence which is something that has to be built. Accept the blame for your own bad actions and see them as an opportunity to learn so you can better yourself. Don't seek to be the center of attention or be desperate for attention from others. This allows you to present your most genuine self.

When dealing with people learn to withstand uncomfortable situations. Running away doesn't allow you to learn to adapt and expand your personal boundaries. Always face the truth no matter how difficult. This allows you to plan your way to a better life sooner rather than later.

38. THE ODD FELLOW'S PHILOSOPHICAL STONE

Knowledge is a stable and mighty stone in a weary land, and three paths travel to it. To seek this stone, one must begin the journey at a sepulcher containing the earth's most dreary and melancholy dust. You will approach the sepulcher through the overhanging darkness of calamity until finally, after a long trek involving doubt and difficulty, light-reveals the three paths. On the first path, you will travel with another who guides you toward the stone, where you learn that those who bow down near it become the monarch of all they survey. On the second path, you travel from high to low. Two will pass, and one of three will show the proper course. On the third path, you are permitted to smite the philosophical stone, and from it gushes fountains of living waters, which form rivers of wisdom, flowing to the uttermost parts of the earth, carrying the idea of a life well lived to the souls of humanity.

From the east side of the stone, the river of science through labor and research flows in a deep, straight course, searching out hidden mysteries, and demonstrating facts.

From the west side flows history, with its broad stream bringing knowledge down through the vanished centuries, revealing many lost arts, which avails us much in these latter days. History unveils mysteries which magicians have left behind them— secrets for ages undusted—so we can read the records of the past.

From the north point on the stone of knowledge gush the sweet fountains of poetry, literature, and music, singing on their way through charming, secluded dells, where there are moss-covered rocks, clinging vines, fragrant flowers, ferns, and singing birds. In their shining waves of light are mirrored the azure sky, golden sunshine, and fleecy clouds, while youth, beauty, laughter, and joy stray along the verdant shores, keeping time to the music of the merry spray and weaving garlands to crown their radiant brows.

On the south side of the stone of knowledge flows a deep stream, calm, clear, and beautiful. Majestically, it sweeps through stately forests, extended plains, and lofty mountains; and the fair cities of honesty, temperance, and truth are built on its shores. This excellent stream is fed by the ever-living fountains of honor, morality, justice, mercy, and divine love.

In a dark, forbidding forest near the stone is the turbid and polluted stream of politics, discontent, and war. Their crimson billows cast wrecks on the strand. The moaning waves strangely blend the tones of martial music with the discords of despair and disappointment, for it is a treacherous tide. Along its winding shores, war builds her forts. There are fields of carnage and blood, and dark fortresses of envy, from which fly the poisoned arrow shafts of hatred, falsehood, and revenge. There are many graves in which lie ambition, glory, and renown, with all their misguided dreams.

39. FINDING OPPORTUNITY IN ODD FELLOWSHIP

Everyone who has the right purposes and plans in line with their abilities and aptitudes has had opportunities available. Every person has had all the opportunities they could use, whether they chose to use them or not. The parable of the talents shows that each person was given money as they could handle it. And so it is with your opportunities. Unique opportunities are for uncommon people. If you live as an average or ordinary person, you cannot expect such opportunities as a genius would have. However, a genius may not have the same opportunities as you.

But, as you know by now, you're endlessly improvable.

There is a place where the average person can be successful in the practice of law, medicine, retail, or anything else. There is room for all people with their varied talents--great and small-- as long as they are willing to use their opportunities. There is no place for a genius or average person anywhere if they aren't faithful to the options available to them. Where the average person is aware of their opportunities, they will rise above the genius. Likewise, if they refuse to recognize their prospects, the genius will fall to the realm of average.

There is opportunity in technology, education, army, air force and navy, the ministry, law, medicine, farming, construction, engineering, sales, and working at manual labor. Not all of nature has been conquered, nor the soil's resources developed, nor all truths discovered, nor all books written. There are not enough people to do it all, even if all were busily at work.

Being active in the lodge creates endless opportunities for those who seek them.

There are three conditions in using opportunities. The first is insight. The primary issue with most people is that it's not that we don't have opportunities, but that we don't see them. Another condition is that you must seize opportunities as well as see them. This readiness requires two things from an Odd Fellow: a focus on looking for opportunities, and the habit of taking action. A third condition is that you do the thing to which opportunity leads thoroughly. This has the habit of making small opportunities into greater ones.

How do you recognize an opportunity? Look for an undeveloped power of nature or technology. Look for a need to be supplied, or any work, production, achievement, or task to be done. These are opportunities. Whenever someone complains about something that needs doing, you have an opportunity. When someone points out that somebody should do something better or there is a problem, you have an opportunity. When someone offers you help, you have an opportunity. When you offer others support, you have an opportunity. One opportunity may have as many rooms as the mind leading to a labyrinth of positive options.

Opportunities abound before you. Learn to see them and learn to act on them.

40. DOING ONE THING WELL

"He who chases two hares catches neither."

The notion of doing one thing well can apply in Odd Fellows to two situations: A) you, the individual, and B) your lodge.

Versatility has its perils. Sure, it's possible to do many things at once, but it makes it very difficult to do all of them brilliantly. Few are the people or lodges who can be versatile in dozens of areas. Few people or lodges can be specialists in two things, especially if they are the opposite. This would require two completely different types of skills. It is a positive weakness to do too many things. Every person or lodge only has so much power. They can run their power into one channel and get energy, or run their power off into several channels and let it waste itself in diffusion. The latter way is the way to gain in breadth but lose depth and momentum.

You should have a vocation or primary type of employment. You should also have a recreation, which would be a hobby and also a minor secondary occupation. The minor occupation should, in some way, tie into your primary vocation, so that you can make use of the same or similar personal skills to be successful. You may find that your hobby can also tie into your vocation. In your career, you must do your work, and in your hobby, you should find your recreation from work and for work.

The power to form and carry out purposes is dependent on the concentration of energy on those purposes. The mark aimed at becomes dim and unappealing if you or your lodge are aiming at many marks. An art, like a vocation, requires the whole heart and life of its devotee. Every calling should be an art into which you can put your whole self.

Doing one thing well leads to the recognition that doing one job at a time is also essential. Doing just one thing at a time helps you remember more, get more done in less time, de-stress, bring more attention to your work, and work smarter, instead of just harder. It's worth the struggle a hundred times over. Doing one small job at a time instead of trying to do several can lead to a feeling of simplicity. Doing several things at once clutters your mind and results in fatigue and overexertion of your mind.

41. THE GOOD SAMARITAN

The story of the Good Samaritan can instruct you in several lessons: How do we overcome religious and ethnic division? What are the differences between ethics and law? How do we deal with our prejudices so we may help another?

Though the law often embodies ethical principles, ethics and law aren't the same. Law is a systematic set of widely accepted rules and regulations created by an appropriate authority such as the government. Laws may be regional, national, or international and governs members of society with enforceable penalties. Law is created by the government to maintain social order and peace in the community and protect all citizens. Violation of the law results in punishment such as imprisonment or fine or both.

Ethics are the principles that guide a person or society, and are created to decide what's good or bad, right or wrong, in a given situation. It regulates a person's behavior and conduct. It helps a person live a good life by applying moral rules and guidelines. Ethics is a guide for necessary human conduct to help people decide right from wrong and how to act. Ethics cannot be enforced like law.

It can be argued that the Independent Order of Odd Fellows is an organization that teaches ethics.

When we study the story of the Good Samaritan, we find that it involves both law and ethics. Those who passed by the injured traveler and refused to help did so because of specific religious and government regulations of the time period. These also bound the Samaritan, yet he decided to do otherwise: he chose to help the injured man. It is here the conflict between ethics and law comes into play. Should doing what's right be a violation of the law? Should the person who does the "correct thing" receive punishment if it violates the law? Philosopher Immanuel Kant believed that what mattered is whether or not the person who helps another does so out of their heart's kindness and does not expect a return favor or reward. Only if something springs from a desire to do good with no expectation for a reward can we say that "goodness" has occurred.

In our version of the story of the Good Samaritan, there were social, ethnic, and religious barriers that existed between Samaritans and Jews, yet the Samaritan eschews these so he can help the injured man. However, the priest and the Levite both chose to avoid the wounded man, possibly because they were in a hurry, or they considered blood religiously unclean, or feared for their own safety, or simply had no concern whatsoever for the man. These issues open up new ethical questions you can explore on your own. Most specifically: under what circumstances will people sincerely do good with no expectation of benefit?

The Good Samaritan parable, found in many wise traditions, asks an Odd Fellow to become more fully human by opening themselves up to examine the prejudices within. It gets you to cross the bigotry line that you may have constructed within yourself: prejudice toward political beliefs, prejudice toward skin color, prejudice toward religion or sexual orientation, prejudice toward gender. It calls you to cross barriers of stereotypes based on external differences to see the humanity in all of us.

The Good Samaritan asks you to embrace an improved society. He encourages you to adopt a fresh world-view, and it is this: *You don't need a victim to abuse to affirm your sense of worth.*

42. CLOSING

You may be poor or face discrimination in a way that makes life even more difficult for you. There are perhaps some unchosen factors in your life that will offer a resistance strong enough to test all your power. But, *you* must make *yourself*-- though there are great difficulties in your way. These strong powers will train your weaker power. You must master these difficulties as much as possible. If you are not entirely determined, they will master you and unmake you.

We, as Odd Fellows, understand that not all start at the same point in life. We illustrate this in the lodge when we acknowledge that we don't recognize the classes of society. In the lodge, we're all Odd Fellows.

Suppose you elevate your point of view toward goodwill, and you are seeking to be true to all that is heroic and great in your nobly-endowed nature. In that case, you're bound to be a successful Odd Fellow by the decree of the universe. You are bound to be crowned, not only with success as society defines it, but success as faith, hope, and charity measures success. You may feel pain; you may feel the slings and arrows of outrageous circumstances; you may experience neglect; you may groan under the pressure and weight of many woes. You may weep bitter, burning, scalding tears of sorrow and grief, but you will triumph. The universe is just and will crown you with perfect equity.

And so, a central truth delivered to you is this: that when you are simply being, then life on the summit of experience is a supreme, resplendent luminary. Not argument, not philosophy, not the elaborate, logical processes of the intellect, but being; this is a great infallible teaching. Live to simply be, and you'll live. Pure sense experience, unmixed with emotional thoughts, is what you seek. All life is in the present. Even when you imagine, or think of the past or of the future there is only one place this can occur: right now. This moment. Knowing this can help you to simply "be."

You are too strong to be defeated, save by yourself. Refuse to live merely to sleep and eat. Animals can do this. You are human. Act the part of a human. Prepare yourself to endure toil. Resolve to rise—you have but to resolve to do so. Nothing can hinder your success if you're determined to succeed. Don't waste your time by wishing and dreaming unless you're laying specific plans and then go earnestly to work. Let nothing discourage you. If you have no books, borrow them. If you have no teachers, teach yourself; if your early education was neglected, be diligent, and repair the defect. Let not a craven heart or a love of ease rob you of the invaluable benefit of self-culture.

Many people plunged into the view that they are predetermined to fail or never be successful. Even though they have more advantages at the start, others believe that they are defeated from the beginning. But, you are an Odd Fellow. And, an Odd Fellow has the support of universal sister and brotherhood. In Odd Fellowship, you'll be supported in your endeavors and encouraged to pursue the life you wish to design for yourself. The Order only asks that you participate. If you do this and do so with an open heart and the desire to help others, the Order's benefits will open opportunities for you. You must work in the Order for it to work for you.

35 QUOTATIONS

"Worrying is carrying tomorrow's load with today's strength-carrying two days at once. It is moving into tomorrow ahead of time. Worrying doesn't empty tomorrow of its sorrow, it empties today of its strength." *Corrie ten Boom*

"Don't let your mind bully your body into believing it must carry the burden of its worries." *Astrid Alaud*

"Don't try to steer the river." *Deepak Chopra*

"People tend to dwell more on negative things than on good things. So the mind then becomes obsessed with negative things, with judgments, guilt and anxiety produced by thoughts about the future and so on." *Eckhart Tolle*

"He who fears he will suffer, already suffers from his fear." *Michel de Montaigne*

"Each morning when I open my eyes I say to myself: I, not events, have the power to make me happy or unhappy today. I can choose which it shall be. Yesterday is dead, tomorrow hasn't arrived yet. I have just one day, today, and I'm going to be happy in it." *Groucho Marx*

"If you want to be happy, set a goal that commands your thoughts, liberates your energy, and inspires your hopes." *Andrew Carnegie*

"Happiness cannot be traveled to, owned, earned, worn or consumed. Happiness is the spiritual experience of living every minute with love, grace, and gratitude." *Denis Waitley*

"If you want others to be happy, practice compassion. If you want to be happy, practice compassion." *Dalai Lama XIV*

"Happiness is found in doing, not merely possessing. *Napoleon Hill*

"Whatever you're looking for is also looking for you. You see, don't only look. Be available and ready when it shows up." *Sahndra Fon Dufe*

"So long as the memory of certain beloved friends lives in my heart, I shall say that life is good." *Helen Keller*

"The friend who can be silent with us in a moment of despair or confusion, who can stay with us in an hour of grief and bereavement, who can tolerate not knowing... not healing, not curing... that is a friend who cares." *Henri Nouwen*

"That was the thing about best friends. Like sisters and mothers, they could piss you off and make you cry and break your heart, but in the end, when the chips were down, they were there, making you laugh even in your darkest hours." *Kristin Hannah*

"Your experiences will be yours alone. But truth and best friendship will rarely if ever disappoint you." *Anne Lamott*

"Remember, we all stumble, every one of us. That's why it's a comfort to go hand in hand." *Emily Kimbrough*

"He that would govern others, first should be the master of himself." *Phillip Massinger*

"Industry pays debts, despair increases them." *Benjamin Franklin*

"You never know how strong you are until being strong is the only choice you have." *Bob Marley*

"I know you can't live by hope alone; but without hope, life is not worth living." *Harvey Milk*

"I have no regrets in my life. I think that everything happens to you for a reason. The hard times that you go through build character, making you a much stronger person." *Rita Mero*

"There's a lot of people out there who go through hard times, and they feel alone. They feel like nobody is there. But I'm in the same boat." *Brandy Norwood*

"Born through hard times, Ghetto child of mine. I wonder if you have to suffer for your father's crimes." *Tupac Shakur*

"From the deepest desires often come the deadliest hate." *Socrates*

"Success makes so many people hate you. I wish it wasn't that way. It would be wonderful to enjoy success without seeing envy in the eyes of those around you." *Marilyn Monroe*

"Hate destroys the very structure of the personality of the hater.... when you start hating anybody, it destroys the very

Think Like An Odd Fellow!

center of your creative response to life and the universe; so love everybody." *Martin Luther King, Jr.*

"Hate is the consequence of fear; we fear something before we hate; a child who fears noises becomes the man who hates them." *Cyril Connolly*

"Quality is never an accident. It is always the result of intelligent effort." *John Ruskin*

"Quality is never an accident; it is always the result of high intention, sincere effort, intelligent direction and skillful execution; it represents the wise choice of many alternatives." *William A. Foster*

"Make the workmanship surpass the materials." *Ovid*

"No one can make us feel inferior without our consent." *Eleanor Roosevelt*

"You can only be jealous of someone who has something you think you ought to have yourself." *Margaret Atwood*

"The most valuable possession you can own is an open heart. The most powerful weapon you can be is an instrument of peace." *Carlos Santana*

"Where justice is denied, where poverty is enforced, where ignorance prevails, and where any one class is made to feel that society is an organized conspiracy to oppress, rob and degrade them, neither persons nor property will be safe." *Frederick Douglass.*

"I feel safe in the midst of my enemies, for the truth is all powerful and will prevail." *Sojourner Truth*

Bibliography

Academy of Ideas www.youtube.com/user/academyofideas

Augustine, Zachary G. *Philosophy For Any Life,* 2015

Aurelius, Marcus *Meditations*

Beharrell, Reverend Thomas G. *The Brotherhood: being a presentation of the principles of Odd Fellowship*

Beharrell, Reverend Thomas G. *The Odd Fellows Monitor and Guide*

Campbell, Joseph *The Power of Myth,* 2011

Colaw, Joshua A. *The Beacon Light or Illuminated Odd Fellowship*

"Does Democracy Demand the Tolerance of the Intolerant?" www.openculture.com

Donaldson, Paschal *The Odd Fellows Textbook and Manual,* all editions

Ford, William Henry *Symbolism of Odd Fellowship,* 1904

Gracian, Baltasar *The Art of Worldly Wisdom,* 1647

Grosh, Aaron Burt *The Odd Fellows Manual,* all editions

Kirtley, James S. *The Young Man and Himself,* 1904

Plato, *The Republic*

Psychology Today www.psychologytoday.com

Psy2Gotv www.youtube.com/user/Psych2GoTv

Ridgely and Donaldson *The Odd Fellows Pocket Companion,* all editions

Ross, Theodore A. *The History and Manual of Odd Fellowship*

Ross, Theodore A. *Odd Fellowship: Its History and Manual*

The School of Life www.youtube.com/user/schooloflifechannel

Wikipedia www.wikipedia.org

www.ingramcontent.com/pod-product-compliance
Lightning Source LLC
Chambersburg PA
CBHW051425090426
42737CB00014B/2827